AARON SHERRITT

First Printing, 2022

For more information go to: www.aguidetoaustralianbushranging.com/

To contact the author, email: australianbushranging@gmail.com

Previously published, in part, on A Guide to Australian Bushranging on 26 June 2020.

Phelan, Aidan
Non-Fiction
Australian history – True crime

ISBN 978-0-6489572-2-5

An entry for this title is available on the National Library of Australia Database

Edited and formatted by Aidan Phelan
Cover designed by Aidan Phelan

Contents

TIMELINE

Aaron Sheritt [i.e. Sherritt], One of the Kelly Gang. (1914).

"It appears that at one time Sherritt was a friend of the Kellies, but was most intimate with Joe Byrne. He had been several times in jail, and on one occasion was convicted with Byrne of stealing a quantity of meat. His father, John Sherritt, an ex-policeman, is a selector, now an elderly man, and resides at Sebastopol, which is about eight miles from Beechworth. The deceased man had a selection of 107 acres about a mile from his father's place, and it is noteworthy that he was assisted in fencing it in by Joe Byrne and Ned Kelly. He was about twenty-four years of age, of robust health, and was noted as a runner and jumper. His holding was on the Woolshed Creek, in the county of Burgoyne, and about two months ago he sold it to Mr. Crawford of Eastern Arcade, who is also a large coach proprietor, and has property to a considerable extent in the district. After selling the land he built a hut at Sebastopol, about two miles away, and it is there he was shot."

"Murder of Aaron Sherritt."
The Goulburn Herald and Chronicle
30 June 1880, P.2.

Foreword

From before the night of Aaron Sherritt's murder on the 26th of June 1880, half-truths concerning his involvement in betraying his lifelong mate and Kelly gang member Joseph Byrne were already widely in circulation among Kelly supporters and residents of the Woolshed Valley. This belief of betrayal has remained at the forefront of much of the literature regarding the Kelly gang in the 142 years since that night in June, but is a viewpoint that is slowly being eroded and questioned, thanks in part to writers and researchers who are willing to delve deeper into the actions and life of the larrikin of Sheepstation Creek. This is no clearer demonstrated than in the work presented by Aidan Phelan in 'Aaron Sherritt; Persona non Grata', where the complexity of Aaron's personality and the role he had taken on was far from black and white.

Within *Aaron Sherritt: Persona non Grata*, Aidan presents evidence that exposes the underhandedness of the true police spies, namely Aaron's brother Jack and his childhood mate James Wallace, and the active part they played in giving information to the police, with much of it incorrectly being placed on the shoulders of Aaron. Furthermore, the unwavering trust Byrne had in his mate, until the erosion of that trust by the poison of those around him, in particular Byrne's mother Margaret, highlighting that there were many others with blood on their hands when the outlaw pulled the trigger on that fateful night in June.

Aaron's motive to protect his mate is clearly presented within the evidence produced by Aidan and will no doubt go on to fuel new discussions around the true role Sherritt played in the 'Kelly outbreak', and also the way in which he so often used the trust placed in him by members of the Victoria Police to protect Byrne. Finally, the title in itself is apt, and a sad reflection on the life of Aaron Sherritt, for during the last few months of his life he had indeed found himself as an outsider to his own family and those he had once been close to.

I feel I should acknowledge how truly honoured I am at being the one chosen to write this foreword for Aidan Phelan's *Aaron Sherritt: Persona non Grata*, as the lives of Aaron Sherritt and Joe Byrne have been a major interest area of mine for most of my life. Over the past five years, this passion has intensified and I have devoted much of my time to researching these two men in order to better understand their lives and actions, and in turn, share this with others, including my partner Aidan. For when you study these people, you begin to understand their goodness, complexities, their faults, their humanity and you are also given a choice. You can either accept what has always been written or said about them, or you disregard these preconceptions and untruths and learn who they were with a clean slate. Or, as Ned Kelly himself so wonderfully put it, "After the worst has been said against a man, he may, if he is heard, tell a story in his own rough way."

Aaron Sherritt: Persona non Grata is a book that gives Aaron Sherritt the opportunity of telling his story in "his own rough way." This book will be a valuable addition to the wealth of Kelly literature and will help to set the record straight on who Aaron Sherritt was and how he became *persona non grata*.

— *Georgina Stones, May 2022.*

Preface

The story of Ned Kelly has taken on mythical proportions in Australian culture and with it many of the people around him have been cast in roles that are often extremely detached from reality in order to facilitate more streamlined storytelling. A prime example of this is Aaron Sherritt, a man who went from one of the Kelly Gang's greatest allies to being portrayed as its greatest traitor, some even going so far as to liken him to Judas selling Jesus to the Romans for a bag of silver.

In books, theatre and film he is usually portrayed one of two ways. He is either a slimy, disingenuous shyster selling information to the police, or he is a happy-go-lucky larrikin who is coerced by the police to give away his mates' secrets for cash. Either way, the common perception is that Aaron Sherritt was a man whose loyalty was only as good as the next pay-out.

Among historians much conjecture has been made around how Aaron Sherritt can be pigeon-holed. Was he a sympathiser who simply fell out of favour? A martyr? A double agent? Or an out-and-out traitor? Most perspectives rely heavily on the same broad brushstrokes and over-simplifications that have plagued popular understanding of the Kelly story for over 140 years. The truth is far more complex than what most people care to acknowledge, and the more one delves into the events of the Kelly outbreak, and Sherritt's role in it, the harder it becomes to slap a label on him. Aaron Sherritt was the kind of person that made friends easily, but by the time he met his infamous death nearly everyone in his life had turned against him. To have people from all sides ostracising Sherritt indicates that many of the presumptions about his character are likely wrong.

In order to truly get to grips with who the real Aaron Sherritt was it becomes important to take a closer look at his life without framing it, as other texts do, as merely a small component of the Ned Kelly story. There were many more years of Aaron's life without Ned Kelly in them than the inverse, and it is somewhat bizarre that this simple fact often gets overlooked. The Kelly saga only really impacted the last three years in Aaron's lifetime, so how does the life he led prior contextualise his behaviour during those turbulent years? That is what this text is about, and in it you will see Aaron Sherritt's life presented in a degree of focus that has not been attempted before. It plucks Aaron out of Ned Kelly's shadow and holds him in the light in all his complexity.

I will take the opportunity here to acknowledge the incredible historical work performed in this area by two people to whom I owe significant debt of gratitude. The first is the late Ian Jones, whose incomparable book *The Fatal Friendship* was the first to explore the role that Aaron Sherritt and Joe Byrne's relationship played in the downfall of Ned Kelly, and from which I began my journey in piecing this book together. I met Ian only three times in my life, all very briefly, and I have a letter he wrote to me that I treasure that really pushed me to pursue this path.

The second person is my partner Georgina Stones, whose research on Joe Byrne is ground breaking to say the least. It was after many terse discussions that she began to research Aaron as well and discovered some of the more obscure facts about Aaron that I have included in this book.

Her ability to find things is absolutely mind-bending to watch and I am very blessed to have her as a research partner as well as a life partner. Her help on this book has been vital to getting it over the line.

There are others who have been a great support to my work, including those who have followed my project A Guide to Australian Bushranging, but namely Noeleen Lloyd whose sage advice is always welcome, and more recently Deb Robinson who has provided opportunities for historians such as myself to have a platform. Both of these women are formidable historians in their own right and are always ready and willing to offer help where they can. You can never overstate the impact of such people in one's life.

Finally, I wish to acknowledge Aaron himself. Without him looking over my shoulder all the time this book would never have come to pass. I felt he was owed a chance to have his story told sympathetically and fairly without ideas being projected onto him. At the end of the day, this book is about remembering a victim of violence and understanding the ripple effects violence creates.

I

Beginnings

The story of Aaron Sherritt begins with John James Sherritt, a member of the Irish constabulary, and his wife Agnes Anne Nesbitt who hailed from County Cavan in Ireland. The couple married at the Church of England chapel in Knockbride on 7 June 1853, coinciding with a period of turbulence in John's professional life. John was a 1st Sub-Constable, but in August he received a demotion. By October he had decided to resign from the constabulary and did so with multiple infractions against his name.

John and Anne Sherritt travelled from Dublin to Liverpool and then on 27 February 1854 they headed for Australia on the *Matoaka* as assisted immigrants. The ship's records indicate they could both read and write. They arrived in Hobson's Bay on 26 May 1854 and briefly settled in Prahran where they were employed by Captain John Harrison.

Their first-born, Aaron Sherritt, was born in August 1855, while his parents were still living in Prahran. Soon after this John applied to procure land under a miner's right, shifting the young family to the north-east of the colony where they took up residence on a patch of land at Reid's Creek in the Woolshed Valley. John did not work as a full-time gold digger, rather attempting to establish himself as a dairyman.

In October 1856 the family welcomed Elizabeth into the world, though she would become better known as Bessie. In March 1858 John James Sherritt, better known as Jack, joined them followed by William George (Willie) in 1860, Anne Jane in July 1862, Julia Frances in August 1864, Esther in February 1867, Mary in August 1869, Maria in May 1872, Martha in July 1875 and Hugh in 1878.

Reid's Creek was a rough and rugged area right in the heart of the goldfields of the north-east of the recently formed colony, Victoria. Here the children attended the Reid's Creek School, and in 1864 the family shifted to Sheepstation Creek a short distance away from a geological structure called Native Dog Peak, though the children remained enrolled at Reid's Creek school. John built a house for his family here and established a small farm. It was not a lucrative pursuit, but it kept the family housed and fed.

Aaron Sherritt was not a very good scholar, seemingly preferring to instead explore the area, where he met a local boy named Joseph Byrne. The two boys immediately hit it off and the pair were almost inseparable, Aaron even wagging from Reid's Creek School to visit the Woolshed Common School; the Catholic school where Joe and his siblings took their lessons. Naturally, the Catholic Byrnes would be wary of Aaron and his family, and the Protestant Sherritts equally wary of the Byrnes, but the friendship between the two boys continued to flourish. However, it was Anne Sherritt's assertion that Joe was a corrupting influence on Aaron. She felt Aaron was too easily led astray and too free with answers when asked questions, which led her to remain wary of the young Catholic interloper who was so often in company with her son.

Now firmly established at Sheepstation Creek, John Sherritt began to expand his land holdings, purchasing blocks around the existing run where he would put his sons to work helping him with upkeep and attending to his sheep, horses, and cattle. Unfortunately, this attempt to set himself up as something of a respectable member of society seemed to bring out the worst in John Sherritt and he became quarrelsome and belligerent, especially towards his neighbour James Kelty and even the local vicar. Such was the animosity between John Sherritt and James Kelty that they would occasionally come to blows. However, in February 1870 John faced court for assaulting Kelty, having attacked him with a large stick and beating him so savagely that he was rendered unconscious. Kelty was subsequently hospitalised when located face down in a ditch, bleeding from the head and unresponsive. Sherritt had handed himself in to Constable Michael Edward Ward, whose name was to become a recurring fixture in the story of the Sherritts, and they rode out to find Kelty still lying where Sherritt had beaten him senseless.

Over the course of several months the case came before the courts in Beechworth, however a verdict could not be agreed upon by the jury and in February 1871 the Crown prosecutor entered a *nolle prosequi* and Sherritt was discharged. It had been a protracted process and had cost the family a considerable amount of money, also forcing Anne and the children to look after the farm themselves while John was remanded without bail for almost five months, awaiting his day in court at the General Sessions.

During this period Aaron would have had to step up into the role of breadwinner, aged fifteen. Such a great deal of responsibility would have weighed heavily on the otherwise carefree teen. It was a pain that was shared by fourteen-year-old Joe Byrne as in November of 1870 his own father died suddenly of a heart attack, leaving behind a widow and seven children.

As teens, Aaron and Joe began to spend much of their downtime in Beechworth, a radiant and ever evolving city that had boomed because of the discovery of large amounts of gold in Spring Creek. It was a place where fortunes were lost as quickly as they were gained, and it was also here that Robert O'Hara Burke worked as a police superintendent in the years before embarking on his doomed expedition to the Gulf of Carpentaria and the local athenaeum *cum* museum was named in his honour in 1862. The prosperous gold diggings had seen a rush of prospectors converge upon the area from Ballarat and Bendigo in search of the elusive yellow stuff, a great number of which were Chinese immigrants. The deeply embedded racism of many European miners led to escalating tensions between them and Chinese miners, resulting in the Buckland Riot of 1857, wherein around 300 drunk white men attempted to expel the Chinese from the region with violence. Chinese men were robbed and beaten, and their tents burned, until the police, under the leadership of Robert O'Hara Burke, broke up the clash.

As with any town with a reasonably large population it was rife with vice and crime. Prostitution, brawling, public drunkenness and stock theft were commonplace in Beechworth and its surrounds. A news report from 1863 illustrates a bizarre incident that is reflective of the nature of life in Beechworth at the time:

"One evening during last week a resident of Beechworth, whose services as an undertaker are frequently put into requisition, having paid most fervent devotions at a shrine where not much water is used, entered one of the hotels in Ford street, and being, no doubt, rather hungry, seized a strong arm of the law with his teeth, the said arm being portion of the body of a member of the police force. He bit right through the constable's coat and shirt, and sent his teeth into the flesh, and, for so doing, was rewarded with a pummelling that will enable him to dispense with any blacking for his eyes for a time to come, and which quickly made him call for mercy."

A PUGILISTIC UNDERTAKING. *LEADER* (MELBOURNE),

5 DECEMBER 1863: 16.

Joe Byrne was known to spend time in the athenaeum reading, Aaron most likely preferring to look at the museum exhibits instead. One of the boys that often accompanied them was James Wallace who was a school-mate of Joe's. As the boys got older and gained more responsibilities, James Wallace became the teacher's assistant to Thomas Trembath at the El Dorado State School, which no doubt took him out of Aaron and Joe's sphere of influence to some degree. He shifted to the Hurdle Creek district in 1873 to assume the role of schoolmaster but it would be far from the end of his involvement in Joe and Aaron's story.

Joe and Aaron were also frequenters of James Ingram's store on Camp Street. Ingram's was a Beechworth institution and he seemed to build a strong rapport with young Byrne, who was keen to utilise the back rooms of the shop to read the paper. Aaron, on the other hand, had no appetite for reading. The two were like chalk and cheese, which somehow seemed to only serve to make them inseparable.

Growing up around Sebastopol, a mining town between El Dorado and Beechworth, gave Aaron and Joe the perfect place to visit when they weren't engaged in chores as it was not so far to travel and there was more excitement. It was a vibrant and intriguing place for a pair of curious teens to explore, but not necessarily one where they would foster good habits. James Bonwick in his book *Notes of a Gold Digger* described the moral state of the goldfields of Australia thus:

"Swearing is an almost all prevailing vice. The reckless-ness begotten by the wild and uncomfortable life, induces this licentiousness of speech. That kind of existence, also, is peculiarly antagonistic to habits of reading and reflection. No retirement is to be found in the tent. Fatigue indisposes one for mental exertion, and there is not the great incentive to reading—a wish to please. The evening's talk is about the work of the day, the probability of success, arrangement for future labor, and, too often, some coarse and spicy anecdote to sustain that excitement of spirit natural to men. No woman's soft voice is there to soothe and to refine. Under no circumstances could I have known better the moral influence of woman in the element of civilization, than in a sojourn at the gold fields. The filth, the disorder, the domestic misery give place at the presence of a female to cleanliness, regularity and comfort. When I passed a tent in which there was a swept floor, a bit of furniture, nicely washed plates, bright pannicans, a sheet to the bed with a clean counterpane over, with here and there a sack or piece of old carpet laid down, I knew that the genial influence of woman had been there. A man once alluding to his home under these circumstances said to me, "you can't tell how comfortable we are." There was a pretty sight to be witnessed at Bendigo; a young, and not an ugly wife, standing under the green bough porch of her tent, playing with a pair of beautiful canaries in a cage."

In Sebastopol, Aaron and Joe would spend considerable amounts of time in the Chinese camp, even earning the nicknames Ah Joe and Ah Jim (because Aaron's name proved too difficult to pronounce.) It seems remarkable that these young men would find themselves drawn to fraternise with a community that was still openly treated by the locals with suspicion, derision and hostility.

Much has been made of Joe's ability to speak Cantonese proficiently, but it is probable that Aaron was also proficient to some degree as he spent time with the Chinese almost as much as Joe, though history doesn't record how robust his linguistic skills were. Aaron certainly was not as academically inclined as Joe and thus it is fair to suggest his level of bilingualism would not be particularly comparable.

In April 1872, Joe became embroiled with a manslaughter case as a witness when two Chinese storekeepers, Ye On and Hung Young, publicly restrained and tortured a man named Ah Suey, who was later found dead as a result of the trauma sustained. Joe gave evidence at the inquest and trial, having seen Ah Suey bound in chains and tied to a post outside the pair's store in Sebastopol, his queue braid hung up on a hook and his body stripped naked below the waist, the wounded man crying loudly. The deceased allegedly owed money to the two storeowners, who may have been linked to the Chinese Triad, a syndicate that was known to provide loans to Chinese immigrants, and frequently implicated in organised crime. The offenders were found guilty of manslaughter and sentenced by Sir Redmond Barry to four years hard labour.

While Joe was working in Sebastopol with the Chinese, Aaron worked on a gold claim with two Chinese men from the Chinese camp named Ah Loy and Ah Fook. Aaron fancied himself as something of a butcher and when his original butcher's licence from September 1872 expired, he tried to obtain a licence under Ah Loy's name that November. The ploy was not as clever as Aaron thought, so when the rort was uncovered by Constable Michael Ward he was fined. Ward was at that point, the superintendent of slaughteryards.

The Ah Fook who worked the gold claim with Aaron and Ah Loy was very likely the same Ah Fook who had been robbed several years earlier by Harry Power, then subsequently assaulted in Greta by a teen-age boy named Edward Kelly, who it emerged had been working as Power's assistant around the time Ah Fook was robbed. It was more than likely that this was also the same Ah Fook whose body was found on the El Dorado Road in May 1874 with his wrists slashed, neck lacerated, abdomen stabbed, and castrated, all wounds apparently inflicted by one of the victim's razors.

Ah Fook seemed to have continued his work sluicing for gold after Aaron had moved on to other pastures, but found himself in debt and got into a fight with another man named Ah On. Both were wounded in the fight, but Ah On was admitted to hospital. By Chinese custom, Ah Fook was required to pay Ah On compensation for the injury, but due to already being in debt was plunged into suicidal depression. Though the Chinese believed that there had been a secret conspiracy to murder Ah Fook, some of the white men tasked with looking at the case seemed assured that it was a case of "self-destruction", though many of the wounds were of such a nature that it was extraordinarily improbable to suggest it was anything other than murder.

Though Aaron had seemingly not fraternised with Ah Fook for two years at that point, there is no doubting that he was aware of the case. Whether it coloured his perception of the Chinese can only be guessed at, but a prominent figure in the case would become a prominent figure in Aaron's own life in a few years.

Another well-known result of Joe Byrne's association with the Chinese was his taste for opium. The drug, though illegal, was frequently smoked recreationally by Chinese men through specially designed pipes. Derived from a poppy flower extract, opium tar was fed into the pipe and heated over a lamp to vaporise it. The result of inhaling the vapour is described as a feeling of bliss and extreme relaxation, but like other opiates it is extremely addictive. In later years Joe's taste for the drug would see him appear in the Chinese camp at Sebastopol to procure it, even though he was one of the most wanted men in the country.

As for Aaron, he seemed satisfied to stick to good, old-fashioned tobacco, though it is probable that he had some experience with opium either through Joe or their mates in the Chinese camp.

As the pair were now almost clear of their boyhood years, there was an expectation that they would act as breadwinners for their families. Joe continued to work odd jobs for the Chinese and various others around the Beechworth and Sebastopol area, while Aaron mostly concentrated on working for his father who was attempting to establish himself as a dairyman. Naturally, this did not leave Aaron with a lot of pocket money and soon he would branch out and pick up odd jobs where he could to earn some extra tin for himself.

Perhaps it was after some coaxing by Aaron, that in September 1873 Joe went onto the common ground that connected the Byrnes to their neighbours and pinched a horse. This particular horse belonged to Anton Wick, a German widower who had been courting Joe's mother. Evidently the young Byrne had starch in his drawers about his potential stepfather and saw no issue with borrowing the black horse with "a tail like any other horse", as Wick described it, which had not been ridden in two months.

Despite Wick's apparent disinterest in riding or working the animal, he took considerable umbrage when Joe borrowed the beast for several days unannounced and returned him steaming hot and saddle sore. It's not hard to imagine Joe riding the black horse to Sheepstation Creek to brag to Aaron about what he just knocked off from Old Man Wick. Aaron and Joe liked to ride their horses hard and naturally the poor animal was ragged by the time Joe had his fill. Wick laid charges against Joe and soon the plucky seventeen-year-old was in Beechworth Court-house facing a charge of illegally using a horse. Luckily for Joe he got off lightly with a fine of 20s plus costs amounting to £1 6s. Butler the magis-trate had some wise words for the young miscreant as well, as reported in the *Ovens and Murray Advertiser*:

> "His Worship said he had not the slightest doubt that defendant had ridden the horse, and he warned him that if he continued this style of riding it would lead him at length to horsestealing. The defendant had better remember that he had rendered himself liable to three months' imprisonment with-out the option of a fine, but in this case, he would inflict a fine, warning him against appearing again on such a charge."

2

Selector & Larrikin

In October of 1873 Aaron began the process of securing a selection for himself. Clearly his time as head of the household in his father's absence while the old man was remanded in Beechworth had given Aaron the confidence to try establishing himself, and in June 1874 he was finally approved.

Becoming a selector was not only a great responsibility, but it was also a heavy burden. Selectors were required to fence and clear the land as well as cultivate it and demonstrate regular upkeep on the property on top of paying monthly rent. Typically, they were forced to work with the table scraps left by greedy squatters that had taken all the prime farmland in an area, which made cultivation extremely difficult even in an area as well suited to pastoral life as the Ovens district. The Victorian Acts in relation to selection that were passed in the 1860s built upon what had previously been established by the New South Wales government under the Robertson Land Acts by putting in more defined terms for those intending to select land for pastoral purposes. This included rates of rent for cattle and sheep, the Board's ability to adjust rent whenever they deem it is excessive or insufficient, and the processes for lodging interest in a run. Rent could be paid in half-yearly instalments, with legal action to be pursued if the rent wasn't paid within seven days of the due date. This would later prove to be a significant issue for Aaron. Parts of the Acts were designed to prevent selectors from squatting on Crown Lands with fines of £5 for grazing stock on Crown Lands without authorisation, £20 for a second offence, £50 for a third, and similar fines for undertaking unauthorised mineral prospecting on Crown Lands to deter would-be prospectors from setting up claims without a license. Additionally, the government had the ability to take land back if they thought they could employ the allotment for mining purposes, with the now-homeless selector compensated financially for the market value of the block. This would mean that Aaron may have worked the selection and established himself there only for the Victorian government to acquire his land from under him on a whim if they believed there was an opportunity to mine for minerals there and he would have to relocate and start from scratch. For Aaron, who was still a teenager and yet to find secure employment, this would all be a tremendous burden to take on.

The selection of 100 acres neighboured that of Aaron's parents. Joe Byrne assisted Aaron and his brother Jack in clearing and fencing and spent so much time there that he was essentially a resident. It was hard work but soon there was a paddock, fences and a small bark hut. It was rough, but it was a home, and from here Aaron could pursue horse-breaking and cattle grazing, which was the only thing the land was really any good for.

At the age of nineteen Aaron made his first court appearance as a witness in a case against James Kelty and his son Daniel. Though he had likely watched many court cases from the public seating, he was now seeing things unfold from the witness stand.

The Kelty father and son duo had stolen and butchered sheep from mutual neighbours, the Mackays, and Aaron had unwittingly helped Daniel Kelty gut the sheep before realising they had been stolen from the Mackays and then refused to take further part in the affair. Given his later proclivities it is quite amusing how adamantly he refused to implicate himself in sheep stealing.

When he took the stand on 30 July, he delivered his account to the court, giving us a glimpse at his gift for telling stories as reported in the paper at the time.

"I am a selector and cattle owner at the Sheepstation, about 150 yards from where prisoners live; I was at their place last Monday morning, about 10 o'clock; Dan Kelty, and his mother, and Jim Kelty were there; I did not see the elder prisoner at that time; I saw Daniel sharpening, and I asked him, "What for?" and he said, "I'm going to kill two or three bloody billy-goats for the pigs;" when I went in to the stable there was a sheep, dead, with the skin off; he asked me to take the inside out, I was a good hand; I did what he asked; while I was doing so, he hauled out another and killed it; he took it from a small lot — some nine or ten; I recognised the second sheep, and told him they were Mr. Mackay's weaners; he said, "Are they?" "Yes," I said, "they are;" "Well," he said, "we'll knock the 'jimmy' off half-a-dozen of 'em;" the "jimmy" is the hide; I then said, "You may knock away; I'm off to look for the mare;" the sheep he hauled out had the red-dagger brand; I did not see any other brand; I went away after telling them they might be caught.

"Daniel Kelty knew I was a good hand at taking the insides out of sheep, by seeing me do it; I only assisted to kill that one on that occasion; the stable had a sort of division, but it has been knocked down; the small lot of sheep were not in the same place as I was; they were in a place on one side attached to the stable; I have been in there twenty times before on business, after harness or one thing or another; I could not see the little lot of sheep without going up to look at them; I cannot recollect whether there is a partition; when I said "These are Mr Mackay's weaners," on seeing one, I saw some others' and went and looked over at them; the stable is lighted by the sun shining through the cracks; "when I saw what they were about, I cleared out;" then I went into the bush, looking for my mare; the prisoners and I are good friends; I have never been in court against them before."

In the end James Kelty was found guilty of receiving stolen sheep and gaoled for four years while Daniel, who it was believed had stolen the sheep then given them to his father, was sent to a boys' reformatory for three years.

By the end of the year Aaron had been well and truly brought into the feud between the two families and was charged with assault against John Kelty after a brawl over some of the Sherritts' goats straying onto the Kelty farm. He was fined £1 and made to pay a £25 bond to keep the peace. This was a nasty knock as Aaron had already been struggling to keep up with his rent payments.

Around the time that Aaron was establishing himself as a selector he fell in with a dodgy pound-keeper, dog catcher, attempted politician and former publican named John Phelan. Phelan was a regular fixture in the courts and the local paper, the *Ovens and Murray Advertiser*, and was almost obsessed with trying to make a name for himself, much to the disdain of Beechworth locals. Phelan had been appointed as Beechworth pound-keeper by the shire in January of 1873 and it is possible that Aaron took up work with him to bring in a bit more money to help him keep up with his rental obligations. He was just one of the local boys that Phelan would use to fetch animals to impound, but Aaron learned a number of tricks that would prove to be very useful to him in later years during this time.

Phelan's confrontational manner, societal aspirations and outspokenness would have reminded Aaron of his father. Phelan was a frequent author of letters to the editor of the *Ovens and Murray Advertiser*, usually attempting to correct some perceived slander or character assassination that had graced their pages — a habit that John Sherritt was also known to partake in.

Under Phelan's direction Aaron was instructed in the most effective ways to steal horses and plant them for retrieval. When the animals were "discovered" by Aaron, under the pretence of having come across them on the loose, Phelan would then impound them. If the owners collected them from the pound the pair would split the pound fee, and if the animals were uncollected, they would sell them for a profit.

Phelan educated Aaron in the techniques used by successful duffers to change or obscure the brands of animals that they had stolen using tweezers to pluck the hairs out, and using a needle dipped in iodine to prick the skin and create the illusion of an old brand.

In November both Aaron and Jack Sherritt went to court, charged with illegally using a horse. It appears a friend of the brothers named John Murphy had come into possession of the horse, a chestnut horse belonging to Henry Sigam, and kept it in a paddock at the Sherritt run at Sheepstation Creek. This strange horse caught the eye of the Keltys who immediately assumed that the horse was stolen but did not report it. In fact, it was Jack Sherritt that rode into Beechworth to report to

Constable Mullane that the horse was stolen and implicated Murphy. Aaron and Jack had evidently heard along the grapevine that the horse was one that was reported as stolen from Benalla and a reward had been offered for it and Jack had decided that the temptation of a reward was just too much to ignore and rode the animal to the police station.

John Murphy would claim that he had merely found the animal, which had gone missing from a railway camp in Everton in September, and rode it to retrieve his own horse. The chestnut, he noted, was quite sore and lame. Both Murphy and the Sherritts had been observed riding the animal as it had been quiet and of a good temperament.

Luckily for the brothers they got off with only a £1 fine each, but behaviours that would come to define their characters in later years were already on display.

Meanwhile, Aaron continued his employment with John Phelan, and in early October he recruited a fifteen-year-old boy named Duncan McAulay to help Aaron impound animals for him. McAulay accompanied Aaron and another boy as they retrieved several horses and took them to the pound. Aaron was riding a chestnut filly with a white face, branded AL on the shoulder. McAulay was guiding an unbroken bay filly. Both horses were the property of Arthur Land of Hurdle Creek who eventually learned that the bay was impounded at Bowman's Forest, the chestnut impounded at Oxley. The indignant farmer, subsequent to paying to release his horses, went to the police. In the meantime, Duncan McAulay had bolted from John Phelan's employ after having only worked with him for three and a half weeks.

When Phelan was questioned by Constable McHugh about the impounded chestnut filly, he was shown an entry in the pound book that stated the horse had been impounded by a man named D. McAulay from Three Mile Creek. When McHugh pointed out that no such man lived there, Phelan then stated that he resided at One Mile Creek. When young Duncan was spotted on the premises the gig was up. Phelan was charged with illegally impounding and falsifying pound records.

Despite all the hard work the police put into sniffing out the crime, they were never able to make all the charges stick, Phelan only being issued fines amounting to £15. The case against Aaron was dismissed due to lack of evidence, though the magistrate did issue a warning to Sherritt that if he was to appear before him again on a similar charge, he would be landed with twelve months imprisonment. It was the first in a series of close calls that began to embolden Aaron, and the authorities would soon learn that when you gave Aaron Sherritt an inch, he would take a mile.

Whatever relief Aaron felt at having dodged gaol time, he evidently was of the impression that he would rather not stick his neck out for John Phelan anymore, and left Phelan's employment around the time of the court case. From now on any transgressions Aaron was to partake in would be on his own steam and he would endeavour to ensure that he was far better at covering his tracks than the irascible pound-keeper.

By some accounts it was around 1876 that Aaron became unofficially engaged to Joe's sixteen-year-old sister Kate, who he had been romantically linked to for some time. One could suppose that the young buck with his own selection and roguish charm must have been quite appealing to a young girl in the blossom of womanhood. In kind, Joe was said to be in a serious relationship with Aaron's sister Bessie, however, Byrne seemed to have had many female admirers around the district and even earned himself the nicknames "Sugar" and "Sweet Birdie". It is difficult to imagine Aaron being content to be "tied down" given his larrikin tendencies, especially in light of the events that were to come.

The relationship with Kate, and the separation from John Phelan, seemed to coincide with a sudden escalation in Aaron's propensity for criminal behaviour and 1876 would prove to be a seminal year in the lives of Aaron Sherritt and Joe Byrne.

On 21 January 1876, Aaron and Joe visited a butcher in Camp Street, Beechworth, named James Warner. With them was a strawberry heifer poley calf (a young female bovine without horns), that they wished to have slaughtered. A deal was struck for Aaron to take the slaughtered animal's hide and head, with the price being deducted from the money the pair were paid for the meat. Aaron stated that he wished to use the hide for making whips.

The Sherritts had a running account with Warner, and he saw nothing suspicious in the transaction, on top of which he was thankful for Aaron to take the head away as Warner had not enough pigs to dispose of it himself. It seemed a fairly open-and-close case until Constable Mullane arrived on the scene in his capacity as an inspector of slaughteryards six days later.

Mullane seemed to suspect that Warner had been dealing in stolen goods and enquired about the heifer. He considered that Warner's account of what had transpired was unsatisfactory and charged him with failing to give a full and satisfactory account of what happened to the hide. It was regulation to keep the hide for a month but between Warner's previous transactions with the Sherritts and the summer heat that would have simply rotted the hide, Warner had not considered it necessary to follow procedure.

When the case went to court, he was fined £5. It was unclear if the heifer that Aaron and Joe had taken to Warner's that day had been acquired legally or not, and the only evidence that could prove or disprove the supposition that it was stolen had been destroyed, presumably to make a whip and some tasty mock-turtle soup.

Soon Aaron and Joe would once again attract police attention over a slaughtered bovine, but this time the circumstances would be considerably different. Apparently, Aaron still fancied himself something of a butcher, and in May he endeavoured to demonstrate his capabilities.

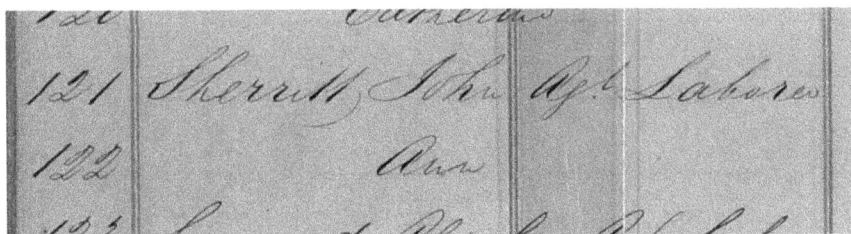

Extract from the shipping registry for the Matoaka showing Aaron's parents as passengers. John was listed as 26 years of age while Ann was only 18.
[Courtesy Public Records Office Victoria, VPRS 14/P0000, Book No.9]

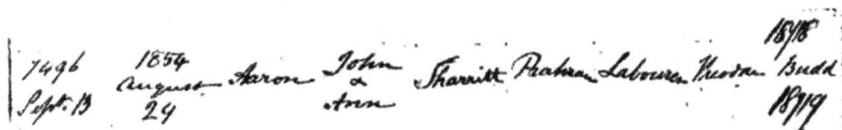

An extract from the Parish of St James baptism records showing Aaron Sherritt's baptism.
[Courtesy: Mick Fitzsimons]

Chinese Sluicing near Beechworth, by N. Chevalier

[Courtesy: State Library Victoria; IAN25/08/64/5]

Sebastopol Flat, former site of the gold diggings where Sherritt and Byrne would visit.
[Author's Collection]

The Woolshed Falls
[Author's Collection]

Ford Street, Beechworth, circa 1875
[Courtesy: Burke Museum, Beechworth; 5570]

3

❦

Concerning a Cow

On 20 May 1876, the pet cow was stolen from the El Dorado Common School by Joe Byrne and Aaron Sherritt. Once it was "liberated", it was then taken to an abandoned and secluded milking yard owned by a man named Edward "Ned" Kennedy, where they would brand animals, or occasionally hold their stolen stock before shifting it. This time, however, Aaron Sherritt's determination to be a butcher seemed not to have diminished in the time since being busted trying to obtain a dodgy licence. Joe borrowed two knives and steel from one of his neighbours, Jane Batchelor, between four and five in the afternoon claiming a cow had gotten stuck in a hole at Limeburners' Flat.

As they were slaughtering the cow were spotted by a local busy-body named Andrew "Sandy" Doig. He stayed long enough to get a good description of the slaughtered beast, which would prove vital in the later court case against the pair, to snidely ask Aaron if he called himself a butcher, and to have the animal's severed tongue waved at him by Aaron.

Once the cow had been slaughtered and bled dry the brand was cut out of the hide, and the carcass was divided into portions that were then divvied up amongst the Byrnes and Sherritts. They both stayed the night at the Byrne selection and then headed off in the morning to take the rest of the carcass to Aaron's parents.

Margret Byrne seemed satisfied with their explanation that the slaughtered beast — of which she had been gifted the head, heart, half the hind quarters and half the fore quarters — was one of Aaron's. When John Sherritt realised what his son had done, on the other hand, he cut the hide into strips and used them to tie a portion of the roof.

On 22 May, Constable Ward and Constable Twomey went to the Byrne selection and seized part of the illegally procured carcass, other parts were reclaimed from Kennedy's yard. Ward, then accompanied by Constable Mullane, headed to the Sherritt farm on Sheepstation Creek the following day where the remainder of the ill-gotten gains were seized. John Sherritt tried to provide an explanation for the meat, claiming one of his own animals had gotten knocked up on the way back from Barambogie and he had killed and butchered it, but the police did not buy what he was selling, particularly when he could not supply the strips of leather that would have filled in the portion of the hide where the brand ought to have been. Subsequently Joe Byrne and Aaron Sherritt were arrested and remanded in Beechworth. With no money to cover the bail, the pair remained locked up in Beechworth Gaol until the conclusion of the trial.

On 30 May the pair went to court on three charges of cattle stealing, but as there was not enough evidence to uphold the charges this was reduced to a charge of illegal possession of a carcass. Any hope that Joe and Aaron had that their luck would hold was quickly dashed as the evidence quickly unravelled the defence. Sandy Doig, Jane Batchelor,

Ned Kennedy, Margret Byrne, Constables Ward and Mullane, and John Sherritt all gave evidence.

By the time John Sherritt took to the stand, the only witness apparently willing to support the defendants, it was already a lost cause. Predictably the pair were found guilty and given the maximum possible sentence for the crime: six months hard labour.

For the first time Aaron and Joe did not leave the dock to head home and breathe a sigh of relief. Instead, they were taken out the back and across to Beechworth Gaol where they were stripped, examined, shaved, bathed, and deloused. They were then given the standard grey woollen prison uniforms and sent to their cells to begin their half a year in Hell. For such young men with no small amount of vanity in their appearance this would have been utterly demoralising.

The life of a prisoner in Beechworth Gaol, as in all Victorian prisons of the time, was not glamorous in the slightest. The granite cells were tiny and sparse, with only a mat made of coconut fibre for a bed, a grey woollen blanket for warmth, a bucket in the corner for the nightsoil (effluent), and a Bible could be read until it was lights out. The summers were boiling and the winters freezing, bathing was done in groups outside in a stone trough, and illnesses were rife. As per the Pentonville model adopted by all mainstream Australian prisons, in Beechworth all inmates wore the same woollen uniforms, heavy leather boots, and white hoods that covered their face when leaving their cell, so they became completely anonymous. As well as being silent when moving from place to place in the prison, inmates wore a calico disc with their cell's number written on it pinned to their chest as their only identification. After their day in the work yard pulverising granite, they would be given a new disc with a new number because every day their cell would change. This made it harder to hide contraband and limited opportunities for inmates to quarrel.

On Sundays the inmates attended mass and there was also a library from which books could be borrowed. Joe Byrne took advantage of this latter fact to write a note that he smuggled out of the prison to Jack Sherritt. By writing on pages torn from a library book he hoped to have Jack bring him tobacco, but the letter was intercepted and reported to the authorities.

Meals usually consisted of bread, water, hominy, oats, and molasses. On Good Friday inmates received fish for dinner. Fresh fruit, vegetables and meat were off the menu.

In November Aaron and Joe gained their freedom, but gaol had done little to curb the pair's flashness or criminal urges. Indeed, prisons in this era seemed remarkably ineffective at doing much apart from breeding even more hardened criminals.

Though history doesn't recall Aaron's feelings about being sent to gaol, Joe Byrne's feelings about the situation that got him locked up for six months would be stated bluntly in the most horrific circumstances four years later.

4

Ah On

January 1877 brought a new year, and one would have thought that would have been an incentive for Aaron and Joe to straighten up with a fresh start. However, only nine days into the year Aaron found himself pulled up on Ford Street, Beechworth, by Constable McHugh. He had been driving a cartload of hay and one of the horses appeared to be in pain and refused to pull no matter how hard Aaron urged it. Upon inspection the horse's shoulders had been rubbed raw. The animals and cart were immediately seized, and Aaron was arrested.

The following day, Aaron appeared in court represented by the Frederick Brown, once again. The afflicted horse was examined, and it was revealed that the collar was so worn out that the hay stuffing was poking through holes in the leather and had skinned the horse's shoulders down into the flesh. Some sacking had been shoved between the collar and the wounds, but the damage was already done. It soon emerged that Aaron had been sent out by his father to sell the hay to Mr. Dennett at the stockyards. Because the hay was left in the rain overnight while Aaron was in remand, it became worthless, and the defence pushed to be compensated for the £4 the hay was worth.

Not only was John Sherritt not compensated for the ruined hay, but Aaron was fined £5, and the wounded horse was confiscated to be sold in satisfaction of the fine if the money was not forthcoming. Magistrate Pitcairn described the case as the most disgraceful he had ever met in his life, and informed John Sherritt that if he had been the driver instead of having sent his son to do the deed, he would have given out a sentence of three months' imprisonment.

On 13 January 1877, Aaron and Joe were involved in an incident against Ah On, a Chinese miner who lived on the outskirts of Sebastopol with two other men named Ah Sing and Ah Seong. The pair had been bathing in a dam near Ah On's house and a dispute arose. While the two larrikins were making their retreat, Aaron threw a rock at Ah On, hitting him in the side of the face, fracturing his zygomatic arch (the bone connecting the cheek between the eye socket and the ear) in five places. Ah On's mates took him to hospital the following day. The wounding was severe and five shattered pieces of bone had to be extracted. The injury was permanent.

A few weeks later the pair were arrested and remanded in Beechworth on assault charges. On 13 February the case went to court for a committal hearing and though the prosecution posed a compelling case, so did the defence. Aaron was once again represented by Frederick Brown and Joe by William Zincke.

Ah On stated in his evidence that he was in the garden that was between the dam and the hut when he saw Joe bathing in the dam with Aaron dressed near him on the bank. Joe supposedly called out to him, though Ah On never indicated if this was a friendly gesture or not. He had known Joe over two years, but Aaron, he claimed, he had only known about ten months, although most of those ten months Aaron had just spent in Beechworth Gaol. Ah On then stated that he went to wash his feet with Ah Seong just outside the hut when Aaron suddenly threw a rock at him but missed. He then stated that he returned to the hut, but Joe and Aaron followed, throwing more stones at him. It was at this time that Aaron threw the stone that injured him. He cried out in pain and Ah Seong chased Joe away with a stick, while Ah On attempted to follow Aaron, also brandishing a stick. Aaron allegedly then threw a stick at his pursuer, but it fell short. After running about 80 or 90 yards, Ah On became woozy and collapsed, bleeding from the head.

When Ah Seong took the stand, he corroborated Ah On's evidence and identified the stone that had injured his mate. Ah Sing had been inside cooking throughout the hubbub and could only testify that rocks had been thrown and that he observed Ah On and Ah Seong chasing the boys with sticks of bamboo.

Dr. Fox, the attending surgeon who had treated Ah On, testified as to the nature of the complainant's injuries as relayed in the *Ovens and Murray Advertiser*'s coverage of the case:

"He had two wounds on the right side of his face, one larger and deeper than the other, and about 3/4 of an inch from his ear. This communicated with a broken bone. The other wound was about an inch from the first and was more superficial. Both these wounds were over the zygomatic arch, composed of bone. Subsequently at the hospital assisted Dr. Farr in removing five pieces of bone from the man's face. These pieces were connected with the wounds described. Prosecutor was still a patient at the hospital. Witness regarded the wounds at one time as dangerous. There was permanent injury done to the prosecutor. He would not be able to masticate as well, and the wound would, no doubt produce disfigurement."

Constable Mullane deposed that he was handed the bloodied rock by Ah Seong, then arrested Joe Byrne on a warrant that same day at Sheepstation Creek. Evidently Joe had elected to stay on Aaron's selection overnight rather than go home. When Mullane informed Joe of the charge, he simply replied, "I did not do it, or see it done."
Mullane then questioned Joe about whether he was at Sebastopol on 13 January and Joe replied that he did not know if it was on that date, but he was present when "the Chinaman got hurt." Naturally this piqued Mullane's curiosity and Joe proceeded to tell him his version of events:

"We were bathing in the dam; when we got out the Chinamen hunted us with bamboos; I ran one way, and Aaron ran the other, and I saw nothing at all of it."

Constable McCracken deposed that he arrested Aaron on the morning of 5 February five miles from El Dorado heading towards Chiltern. Whereas Joe's response had been to plead innocence, Aaron was unabashed:

"I admit the charge; he ran after me and struck me first, and I then struck him with a stick."

The prosecution case was a serious one, but the defence had their own version of events to be heard. The first witness for the defence was Joe's mother, Margret.

Her recollection was that on the night of the assault she, along with Anne Sherritt and the rest of the Byrne children, saw Ah On chasing Aaron with a bamboo stick about 50 yards from his hut and strike him several times. Aaron then, by her account, picked up a stick and threw it, striking Ah On in the head and knocking him down. Meanwhile Ah Seong had chased Joe about 200 yards, before heading back for his mate. He picked up Ah On's bamboo and the stick Aaron threw before helping Ah On to his feet.

Anne Sherritt was next to testify, corroborating Margret's story. She went further to explain that there were still bloodstains on the bridge from Ah On.

Aaron's brother Willie, then only thirteen, corroborated his mother's evidence verbatim, only adding that the attack was instigated by the Chinese men. Given the similarity between his account and his mother's it was assumed he was merely reciting a scripted account and although the evidence could not be withdrawn it was considered essentially worthless.

Mary Byrne, aged twelve, testified in defence of her brother and corroborated the account put forward by Margret Byrne and Anne Sherritt.

The evidence against the defendants was deemed serious enough to go to trial and they were bailed at £50 and two sureties of £25 each.

On 28 February at the Beechworth General Sessions, Aaron and Joe pleaded Not Guilty to the charge of unlawfully wounding. They were arraigned to appear in court and the jury sworn in. The court was then adjourned until 1 March.

When the trial resumed there were no major revelations, although some elements of Ah On's story seemed to change. Now he claimed he had known Joe for over ten years and Aaron "a few months", and that Aaron had thrown a stone at him when Joe had first caught his attention as he was watering the vegetable garden. Apart from some minor detail being added to the account as relayed at the committal, Ah On stated that Joe Byrne had been in the habit of pelting his hut with stones in the past and that he did not see any of the defence witnesses on the occasion.

Constable McCracken's evidence was slightly different this time as well, but in a crucial way. He stated that he arrested Aaron while he was stripping bark from a tree, and when he questioned Aaron about the incident, he had informed McCracken that Ah On had chased him before he attacked. As innocuous as this seems, this small detail was in essence the difference between an unmotivated assault and an act of self-defence.

When Margret Byrne took the stand, she repeated her evidence from the committal, but further questioning highlighted that the dam did not belong to anyone and that the stick Sherritt supposedly used on Ah On was two yards long and thick as a man's leg.

Willie Sherritt's evidence also highlighted a potential conflict over the dam, stating that Ah On had ordered Joe and Aaron, who were both bathing in it, to get out. Willie then went on to state that Ah Sing and Ah Seong both chased Aaron and Joe and beat them with bamboo until their arms bled. He described the stick Aaron threw at Ah On as being "thick as your wrist."

It took the jury just under two hours to deliberate and Joe Byrne was found not guilty outright, but they initially found Aaron Sherritt "guilty of a common assault, committed in self-defence." The judge was unsatisfied with the verdict as it was not clear enough to provide grounds for a conviction and the jury was ordered to make their decision again. This time they returned a verdict of Not Guilty.

It is difficult to say with certainty the exact nature of what happened on that day at the dam, but it certainly seems as if there must have been some degree of animosity between Ah On and Joe Byrne.

It is almost certain that the Ah On in this case is the same Ah On who was hospitalised after a fight with Ah Fook just prior to the latter's horrific murder and mutilation in 1874. If so, it is possible that Ah On and his mates were living apart from the rest of the Chinese community due to being ostracised, and no doubt Joe's Chinese friends would have been in his ear about them. It is also worth considering that if the Ah Fook who was found murdered is indeed the same man that Aaron had mined with, then it is very probable that Ah On's conflict with Ah Fook would have been known to Aaron and this may have played a part in any animosity between them. Alas, we can only speculate.

Perhaps it was merely a case of bored young men getting their kicks by annoying an irascible Chinese man, and the situation going too far, but unfortunately the injuries that Ah On carried after that day would never fully heal, leaving him with permanent impairment to his oral functions and a noticeable crater in the side of his face. It was manifestly unjust, but that was the reality of life among the whites for many Chinese in Australia of the time.

It is possible that while on remand in Beechworth for the assault trial Joe Byrne and Aaron Sherritt first met a teenager from Greta named Daniel Kelly, who was waiting to go to court on 28 February over an allegedly stolen saddle. His big brother Edward, better known as Ned, was in attendance as a witness for the defence. These two sons of an Irish convict and his settler wife were well known to police in that district as juvenile offenders. Ned himself had only recently come out of gaol after doing the majority of a three-year sentence for feloniously receiving a horse, having gained an early release by remission.

Previously, Ned had done six months in Beechworth Gaol as a fifteen-year-old for assaulting a hawker named Jeremiah McCormack and sending an offensive parcel to his wife. The parcel had contained a pair of severed calf's testicles and a note instructing the woman to give them to her husband so he could use them as the couple were childless. Though the note had been penned by a rival hawker named Ben Gould, Ned had forwarded the article to the hawkers via his cousin Tom Lloyd, who had informed the recipients that it was from Ned. Naturally a fight ensued, in which Ned allegedly tried to trample McCormack with his horse.

Ned had a reputation with the authorities, having been identified as an assistant to the bushranger Harry Power in 1869. The charges did not stick as there was insufficient evidence when the cases went to trial. Ned was later arrested for assaulting a Chinese man named Ah Fook, very probably the same Ah Fook that had worked the gold claim with Aaron. Ned also managed to get off in this instance due to insufficient evidence of his guilt. On top of these incidents, he was widely suspected of stealing horses and cattle, planting them, then "finding" them for the rewards offered.

Daniel Kelly, however, had no convictions to his name, but he and his older brother Jim had been arrested in 1871 and held in the Greta and Wangaratta lockups for illegally using a horse. Due to their age, and the fact that the horse belonged to Jim's employer, the case was thrown out and the boys were set free. Daniel was only ten years old at the time, Jim was twelve. Dan was also suspected of having engaged in stock theft, as his brothers and uncles were, but nothing could ever be found to link him to any crimes.

In the case of the allegedly stolen saddle, Dan avoided conviction due to being able to produce receipts for the sale of the aforementioned item. Mounted Constable Robinson testified that he had seen Kelly with the saddle, and when asked to account for how he came upon it, Kelly replied he had bought it from one man and then again from another. Additionally, the manufacturer of the saddle, Edward Shortell, testified to having sold it to Kelly over two years prior, and multiple witnesses, including Ned, testified to having witnessed Dan sell the saddle to a man named Roberts for a pound.

In the end, Judge Hackett threw the case out, stating that the young Kelly had given a perfectly fair account of how he came by the saddle, and that he saw no reason why he should have been on trial at all.

Though Dan had gotten off, Aaron and Joe were still waiting for their trial as it had been adjourned until the following day. It is important to note that there is no definitive account of how Aaron and Joe met the Kellys. As they tended to move in different circles, owing to Beechworth's distance from the Kellys' stomping ground in Greta, it is unlikely that they had made significant contact before this time in Beechworth, but not impossible. It is not difficult to imagine that having met Dan in Beechworth, they may have attempted to reconnect with him after the trial. Regardless of the way in which they met the Kelly brothers, what is unquestionable is that in a matter of months after the Ah On assault trial their lives would be inextricably intertwined.

Interior of the Beechworth Courthouse - where Aaron Sherritt, Joe Byrne and many of their family and associates frequently found themselves as complainants, witnesses or defendants.
[Author's collection]

The Beechworth Heritage Precinct as it appears today. The courthouse is in the centre, next to the telegraph station. At the rear is the lockup and police paddock.
[Author's collection]

Aaron Sherritt's prison record.
[Courtesy: Public Records Office Victoria; VPRS 515/P0000]

Interior view of Beechworth Gaol, where Aaron Sherritt and Joe Byrne
did time over the Eldorado cow incident.
[Author's collection]

The remains of the Beechworth lockup.
[Author's collection]

The site of the El Dorado Museum is the former common school from where Aaron and Joe stole the cow that they butchered, which ultimately landed them in gaol.
[Author's collection]

AARON SHERRITT and Joseph Byrne, see *Discharged prisoners* list, 23rd November 1876, are charged, on warrants, with inflicting grievous bodily harm on Ah On, Sebastopol, Beechworth, on the 13th instant.—O.393. 22nd January 1877.

A clipping from the Victoria Police Gazette regarding warrants for Aaron and Joe related to the Ah On case.

[Source: Victoria Police Gazette No.4 (1877), 24 January 1877.]

SUB-INSPECTOR WARD.

Michael Edward Ward in later life.

[Source: The Herald, 05 December 1905, p.3]

Panorama of Beechworth by the American & Australasian Photographic Company, c.1870s
[Courtesy: Mitchell Library, State Library of New South Wales; IE1250589]

5

Wholesale Horse Stealing

Going back to the convict era there had been staunch advocates for prison reform, but it was a voice of dissent easily ignored by the ruling class. By the 1870s calls for prison reform started to come again, but not all of them were from compassionate voices taking pity on people hardened and brutalised by the system. There were many critics taking aim at the fact that prisons were not as effective in stamping out the flashness of the criminal class and beating them into shape as desired. As the *Australasian* put it in 1872:

> "If the number of criminals could be reduced it would be a most desirable end. But failing that, the next best is to reduce the amount of crime. At the same time, it is an end that is more fully within the scope of the agencies we are able to employ. We can bring influences to bear that will frighten criminals, but are by no means so sure of our power of reforming them. And it is quite clear that this is not done while criminals are better housed and

AARON SHERRITT - 53

fed, and enjoy a higher degree of comfort, than honest labourers can obtain by hard work."

It is an impossible equilibrium to find with a *one-size-fits-all* system: break men completely and they no longer function, but don't break them enough and they just go on to become recidivists. Few embody this better than Aaron Sherritt. He was naturally a larrikin and a thrill seeker. For him, few things gave him more of a buzz than stock theft and his brief stints in Beechworth Gaol did nothing to diminish that. In fact, he would later confide in Superintendent Francis Augustus Hare:

> "Mr. Hare, do you think, if you got me the best mares you could buy, and got me the best entire horse you could purchase, that I could withstand the temptation of taking my neighbour's horses and selling them? No, I could not, no more than fly."

So, naturally, when the opportunity arose in June 1877 to take some local squatters down a peg by stealing their prized horses and selling them, Aaron didn't stop to think twice and joined Ned Kelly, along with Joe Byrne, in a horse stealing racket. Kelly himself would boast a tally of 250 horses stolen, though nothing official exists to back up the claim as they were so good at covering their tracks. The ingenuity of criminals is often as astounding in the simplicity as much as the intricacy of its inventions.

A rotating roster of larrikins from the "Greta Mob", a youth gang from the Kellys' home turf made up mostly of their cousins and a few friends, helped the thieves shift the stolen animals. The operation saw the gang moving stock throughout Victoria and parts of southern New South Wales, specifically between Wagga Wagga and Albury. No doubt Aaron was able to use some of the tricks he had learned from John

Phelan to help disguise the stock, some of which he described to Superintendent Hare, which the officer recounted in his memoirs:

> "Supposing a horse was branded H on the near shoulder, they would turn the H into a H B (conjoined) by getting a pair of tweezers, pulling out the hairs to make a B, and then prick the skin with a needle dipped in iodine. This burns up the skin, and for about a month afterwards it looks like an old brand; new brands were also put on in this fashion, and they could never be detected."

Ned Kelly and Joe Byrne assumed pseudonyms while undertaking the next stage of the operation after the theft. Kelly would be known as "Thompson" and Byrne as "Billy King". One of them would take the stolen and rebranded animals to a town where they were unknown and keep them in a squatter's stockyard pending a sale with a stranger they were scheduled to meet there. "Thompson" (Ned Kelly) and "Billy King" (Joe Byrne, or possibly Ned's stepfather George King) would do the deal – the one "selling" the animals to the other – and a receipt would be drafted up and witnessed by the unwitting squatter, all seeming to be perfectly legal. Thus the "buyer" could take the stock back to Melbourne and have plausible deniability in the event that the stolen animals were recognised, preventing an arrest. Thus, the duffers had nothing to lose and everything to gain.

The Kelly horse stealing racket was a slick operation that managed to start and end without ever being sprung until well after the offenders had pulled the proverbial plug.

However, very little thought crossed the minds of the expert horse thieves regarding the ripple effects of their enterprise on the buyers of the stolen horses that they were selling, and in fact those hens would very quickly come home to roost.

In late 1877 the Victoria Police charged William and Gustav Baumgarten, Samuel Kennedy, William Cook and John Studders with offences related to horses stolen from James Whitty, a squatter Ned Kelly had a particular gripe with.

William Cook was found guilty of two counts of stealing and one of receiving, copping concurrent sentences of six, one and eight years. Samuel Kennedy was sentenced to six years in prison for receiving, William Baumgarten was given four years for receiving, and the others were discharged. Later on, the mysterious "Thompson" would be suspected of being an alias for Ned Kelly, but by then it was too late to act on these suspicions. Ned would even admit in his Jerilderie letter to having stolen and sold Whitty's horses to Kennedy and Baumgarten:

> "The pick of them was taken to a good market and the culls were kept in Peterson's paddock and their brands altered by me. Two was sold to Kennedy and the rest to Baumgarten, who were strangers to me and I believe honest men. They paid me full value for the horses and could not have known they were stolen. No person had anything to do with the stealing and selling of the horses but me and George King. William Cooke who was convicted for Whitty's horses was innocent. He was not in my company at Peterson's."

When Aaron would reflect on those days, he would only mention himself, Joe and Ned. It is impossible to know why Ned's stepfather George King, or indeed any of the other family members and associates linked to the enterprise, had been left out of Aaron's recollections if they were involved at all.

It is generally accepted that George King was involved, largely due to Ned Kelly implicating him in the Jerilderie letter. Kelly stated that the match to the powder keg was when a policeman named Farrell had stolen one of George King's horses and planted it in James Whitty's paddock. King seemingly vanished from history around the time of the larceny, leaving nothing behind but unanswered questions and three small children for his Ellen Kelly to raise.

Certainly, the police had their theories about who had been involved in the exploits of Kelly, Byrne and Sherritt, but nothing concrete to lay charges against any of them, though they had begun to suspect Ned Kelly was involved.

It has been assumed by most historians and biographers that Dan Kelly was part of the syndicate, with Isaiah "Wild" Wright, Tom Lloyd, and Steve Hart being other names that are usually connected to the operation, but it is only speculation. With no charges being laid against them it is a good indication that any evidence was too weak to pursue. Regardless of who was involved, the thieves needed people to help them shift the beasts from place to place without attracting police attention, so it seems probable that many of their friends and family were involved to some degree, and these people would become extremely important to Ned and Joe in the coming years.

6

Everything Changes

Though Aaron would still spend much of his time with his partners in crime, very soon the dynamic would shift considerably.

On 15 April 1878, Ned and his brother Dan went into hiding after a police constable named Alexander Fitzpatrick was injured at their mother's house. Though Ned insisted he was not even there, the trooper claimed that Ned had shot him in the wrist while he was attempting to arrest Dan for horse stealing. It would later emerge that the warrant issued for the arrest of Dan Kelly and his cousin Jack Lloyd had been based on a case of mistaken identity and would not have held up in court anyway. A separate warrant had also been issued for Ned on suspicion of horse stealing at the same time, indicating that the police had come across compelling evidence of his involvement in the recent large-scale larceny, but there was now a more serious warrant out for Ned's arrest on a charge of attempted murder, with a reward of £100 issued for his capture. Dan was wanted for aiding and abetting. Their mother Ellen, their brother-in-law William Skillion and neighbour William "Brickey" Williamson were all arrested and later convicted in relation to the incident. Ellen, with a newborn, was gaoled for three years; the men were given six years each.

In response to the obvious likelihood of arrest, Ned and Dan had retreated to a hideaway in the Wombat Ranges. Their chosen spot was an abandoned miner's hut on Bullock Creek that Dan had taken possession of. Ned decided that they would prospect for gold and make bootleg whiskey in an attempt to raise funds for their mother's legal defence.

Joe Byrne would frequently visit the hideaway in the Wombat Ranges and help the Kelly brothers out. It is unknown if Aaron also visited, though it is likely that he had done so in the half-year during which the brothers had taken up residency there.

They had two separate hideouts; the old miner's hut that belonged to Dan, which lay downstream, where they kept the supplies for the whiskey still; and a fortified log hut upstream, that had been built, apparently on Ned's instructions, to withstand a siege. The walls of this second hut were made of thick, intersecting logs with small holes a rifle could be aimed through, and the door was made from a sheet of steel ballast from a ship, which made the lair ostensibly bulletproof. It was clear that Ned expected armed forces to attempt to capture him and he was prepared to fight them off. It was possible that the Kelly brothers could hold off an attack from within this fortified hut for several days before running out of supplies.

It is worth noting that in an effort to reduce his six-year sentence, William Williamson tried to give information to the authorities that not only exonerated himself, but implicated Joe Byrne as the man Fitzpatrick had mistaken for Skillion, despite the men being different ages and having no physical similarity to each other to justify claims of mistaken identity.

No doubt, Byrne's known association with the Kellys could have been seen as a reasonable excuse for him to have been present, though there is no other corroborative evidence to suggest that what Williamson stated was true. Thus, Byrne's presence in the Wombat Ranges was clearly voluntary, not the result of him trying to avoid arrest over the Fitzpatrick incident or the horse stealing, for which the police seemed to have not suspected him or Aaron.

On 25 October a party of police were sent out from Mansfield to track Ned and Dan in the Wombat Ranges. The party consisted of Sergeant Michael Kennedy and constables Thomas McIntyre, Thomas Lonigan and Michael Scanlan. Kennedy led the group through the bush to a clearing along Stringybark Creek where they set up camp that evening.

Unbeknownst to the police, they had been found by Ned Kelly who had spotted their tracks while scouting the area. Dan Kelly subsequently managed to locate the police camp, but no action was taken. Though the reason for their presence is unrecorded, Joe Byrne and Steve Hart were both with the brothers at Bullock Creek.

The following morning Kennedy and Scanlan rode out to search the area for the brothers, leaving Lonigan and McIntyre to look after the camp. Late in the morning McIntyre took a shotgun and attempted to shoot some parrots. The sound alarmed those at the Kelly hideaway less than a mile away. Oblivious to their proximity to the Kellys, or the fact that McIntyre had now alerted them to the location of the police camp (if they didn't already know), McIntyre set about baking bread in a camp oven while Lonigan read the newspaper.

Ned decided to respond by storming the camp, stealing the weapons, supplies and horses, then sending the police back to where they had come from. Ned would later express that he believed there were other police parties on their way to capture him and that his best chance at survival was to disarm the Mansfield party and use their weapons for themselves in the event of a siege.

Just after 5:00pm, the two Kellys, Steve Hart and Joe Byrne emerged from the tall grass and ferns surrounding the camp, having spent some time watching the police from cover. The police were ordered to put up their hands and were covered by the gang's firearms. Ned was armed with a clumsily modified carbine, Dan had a rifle, Steve had a shotgun and Joe carried an old-fashioned rifle with a large bore. McIntyre put his hands out and Lonigan retreated, clutching at his revolver.

As Dan, Joe and Steve kept McIntyre covered, Ned turned rapidly and fired. McIntyre flinched but did not dare take his eyes off the bush-rangers. The warped muzzle of Ned's weapon discharged a quartered lead ball that split apart into tiny pieces of deadly shrapnel. A piece of shrapnel pierced through Lonigan's left forearm and lodged in the outside of his left thigh. The rest of the pieces sliced across his right temple and punched through the orbital bone of his right eye into his brain. Lonigan reeled and staggered, tumbling to the ground gasping "Oh Christ! I'm shot!"

Lonigan breathed with shallow, laboured breaths as he heaved and plunged into the dirt until, finally, he was still. Within a moment Mounted Constable Thomas Lonigan was dead, aged thirty-two, leaving behind a pregnant widow as well as a son and three daughters.

Ned strode over and inspected the corpse muttering, "What made the fellow run?" as if unable to comprehend how seeing a man approaching him with a gun could have instilled enough fear to cause flight.

Dan said in disbelief, "He was a plucky fellow; did you see how he went at his revolver?"

It remains a matter of debate as to which account of Lonigan's death is more accurate – Ned's or McIntyre's. Ned would maintain that Lonigan had gone behind a log and was coming up to fire on the gang when he was shot. McIntyre was of the opinion that Lonigan did not have enough time to run to cover as Ned stated. The wounds Lonigan received indicate that he had his left side towards Ned and was probably looking over his left shoulder when shot, neither confirming or denying either of the witness accounts.

McIntyre in that moment was overwhelmed but would later state that he did not believe the bushrangers had descended upon the camp with the intention to take life, however Ned's actions in those brief seconds had forced upon them all a situation that would inevitably result in murder.

The gang proceeded to raid the tents and Joe Byrne elected to spend his time with McIntyre. Dan suggested handcuffing the policeman, though this was instantly rebuffed by his older brother who believed the threat of being shot was incentive enough for McIntyre not to disobey him. Ned soon demonstrated incredible agitation, pacing around, and ranting about how all of this was Constable Fitzpatrick's fault. McIntyre was able to take detailed observations of the gang that he recounted in his witness testimony and, later, his memoirs. His impression of Joe was that he was quite different from the other three gang members:

> "Byrne brought up our billy of tea and filling some into a pannickin [sic] he handed me a drink. I thought he did it from a kindly motive but Kelly put a different construction upon his act by asking me if there was any poison about the place. [...] Having satisfied their appetites, Byrne seemed to view my position in a more rosy light than I did myself, for he addressed me as mate and asked if I smoked. I replied in the affirmative and at his request for a pipeful of tobacco I supplied him with a cake which I fully expected to be appropriated but after passing into the hands of

Ned Kelly it was returned to me with an invitation from Byrne to fill my pipe and have a smoke.

Byrne was the only one of the party that spoke to me in anything like a kindly manner during the time I was a prisoner yet he shot at me as I escaped and followed up on my trail for over an hour to murder me."

The gang made short work of McIntyre's freshly baked bread with compliments to the baker, which gave him a slightly perverse sense of satisfaction. Ned spoke at length with McIntyre who made a point to mention that his life was insured, and he had no beneficiaries in Victoria in the event of his death. Ned instructed McIntyre to force Kennedy and Scanlan to surrender to him so that no further blood should be shed. The mood seemed to simmer down somewhat until the returning police could be heard approaching the camp. The gang hid and McIntyre confronted his colleagues.

There was confusion as McIntyre informed Kennedy that he had best surrender as they were all surrounded. Kennedy responded by putting his hand to his holster, whereupon the gang emerged with a shot and announced they were bailing the police up. A gunfight ensued wherein Constable Scanlan was shot dead by a shot from Ned Kelly that passed through his ribs and punctured his lungs, Dan Kelly was shot in the shoulder by Kennedy, and Ned pursued Kennedy into the bush and mortally wounded him.

McIntyre escaped on Kennedy's horse, but after being knocked out of the saddle decided to hide in a wombat hole overnight and walk into town the following day. As McIntyre fled Dan Kelly called out for the gang to shoot him. Joe and Steve pursued the constable into the bush but soon gave up the chase when he could not be found.

The fate of Sergeant Kennedy is a hotly debated point. The only first-hand account of Kennedy's death comes from Ned Kelly, who insisted that after mortally wounding him during their battle he performed a mercy killing. Ned refused to include the presence of Dan, Joe or Steve in his accounts of this moment, though a version of the event that began to circulate by word of mouth stated that Ned sat talking with Kennedy for two hours before Dan and Joe convinced him to finish the sergeant off, as they needed to get moving. Regardless of what exactly transpired, Kennedy was killed by a shot fired at close range, leaving a fist-sized hole in his chest, and his body was covered with a cloak before being abandoned in the bush and left to the mercies of decay and wild animals.

The gang then picked the camp clean and looted the bodies. Joe Byrne took rings from Lonigan and Scanlan as well as Lonigan's watch. The single tent that the police had brought was burned, and the bushrangers headed back to their hideout, which was later found burnt out and abandoned. Within the next twenty-four hours they set out to try and cross the Murray into New South Wales, where the Victoria Police had no jurisdiction.

News of the killings sent shockwaves through the colony, as there had never been a worse singular case of police deaths on duty in the history of Victoria to that point, and the only comparable event was the murders of four special constables in Jinden, New South Wales, in the 1860s that were alleged to have been committed by the Clarke bushrangers. Police parties immediately went out in pursuit of the murderers, and a posse of police and volunteers led by Sub-Inspector Pewtress and Constable McIntyre, who was still badly injured after his ordeal, went out to Stringybark Creek to retrieve the bodies of the slain officers. Sergeant Kennedy's was the last corpse to be discovered, and by the time it was found it was already in an advanced state of decomposition and had been gnawed at by animals.

Meanwhile the gang were on the move. Due to recent rains the Murray was in flood and the punt that would have taken the gang across the river had become submerged, so they spent several days attempting to outrun the police while seeking shelter and supplies.

In the end there was one person that Joe knew they could turn to for help, and around 3 November they rode to Sheepstation Creek to meet up with him.

On a rise behind the Sherritt selection the fugitives fired eight times into the air to raise Aaron Sherritt's attention. Joe's lifelong mate had no hesitation in providing assistance. He got them food and escorted the soon-to-be-outlaws into the bush and guarded them while they slept in the cave at Native Dog Peak where he and Joe would hide out in their early stock thieving days. They remained here for around three or four days before the gang had recovered enough to move on.

Importantly, at this point only Ned and Dan had been identified, based on their resemblance to their known descriptions and a mugshot taken of Ned in Pentridge Prison. McIntyre was not familiar with Joe Byrne or Steve Hart, neither having been linked to the Kellys at the time, and thus could only provide their descriptions as they were not referred to by name during the time that the gang had the police camp under their control. Therefore, Joe and Steve could move around more easily as they were not yet officially named as Ned's accomplices. That would soon change, however.

It is likely that Aaron's exclusion from the gang's ranks was merely a quirk of fate, for Sherritt himself would go on to state that Byrne and Hart had only found themselves involved by accident. It would be very unlikely that Sherritt had not been visiting his mates in the Wombat Ranges in the lead up to the tragedy at Stringybark Creek.

Sherritt seemingly found it difficult to believe that his bosom buddy, or the Wangaratta jockey, would have willingly shed blood, going so far as to tell Superintendent Hare in one of his many heart-to-hearts that Ned Kelly had ordered them to fire into Kennedy's body to prevent them turning informer against him. He would claim Kelly had told him this himself, though this contradicts the story that Ned Kelly personally told whenever given the opportunity, as recorded by myriad witnesses and letters. Once again, there is not enough reliable evidence to suggest the truth of the claim, though Hare was satisfied that the existence of powder burns on Kennedy's skin was enough evidence to validate the story.

One can only speculate about how he felt about Joe getting mixed up in the mess the Kellys had caused. If they had any deep, heart-to-heart conversations about it, then what they discussed was never recorded. What is clear is that, at this early stage, Aaron's sympathies were clear cut, and there was no hint of an inclination towards dobbing in his mates for reward money, let alone any indications of the controversies that were to come on his account. Aaron Sherritt was unambiguously a sympathiser, and an important support for the budding bushrangers.

Joe Byrne photographed in Beechworth prior to his outlaw days.
[Public Domain]

This portrait is believed to be George King and was incorrectly labelled "Joe Byrne". It is easy to see why this might be mistaken for Joe based on later images of him.

[Courtesy: State Library Victoria; 1793729]

EDWARD AND DANIEL KELLY, THE OUTLAWED BUSHRANGERS.

These likenesses were printed after the police murders. The portrait of Ned is based on a mugshot taken when he was 15 with a beard added.

Source: *The Illustrated Australian News, November 28, 1878. [Courtesy: State Library Victoria; IAN28/11/78/196]*

STEPHEN H'ART.

This portrait of Steve Hart was also based on a photo, but had a beard
added to make him look more like a bushranger.

*Source: The Illustrated Australian News, July 17, 1880. [Courtesy: State Library
Victoria; IAN17/07/80/117]*

"Attempted Surprise" from The bush ranging tragedy: scenes and incidents. This illustration depicts the farcical Rat's Castle Fiasco.

Source: *The Australasian Sketcher, 21 December 1878. [Courtesy: State Library Victoria; A/S21/12/78/149]*

SUPERINTENDENT NICOLSON.

Superintendent Nicolson
Source: *The Illustrated Australian News, July 17, 1880.*
[Courtesy: State Library Victoria; 1760663]

Superintendent Hare
Source: The Illustrated Australian News, 3 July 1880.
[Courtesy: State Library Victoria; IAN03/07/80/101]

The Commercial Hotel, Benalla; former residence of Superintendent Hare during the Kelly pursuit.
[Author's collection]

7

The Rat's Castle Fiasco

News of the gang being spotted near the Sherritt property reached the
police after their informant had immediately gone into Beechworth and
spent several days getting blind drunk, ending up in the logs until sober
enough to report. In response, Chief Commissioner Frederick Charles
Standish organised a party of thirty police and civilians to accompany
himself, Assistant Commissioner Nicolson and Superintendent Sadleir,
the man in charge of the district, as they attempted to raid the area
in search of the gang. They were also accompanied by the informant,
who had since disguised himself in blackface to avoid recognition by the
bushrangers, an Aboriginal tracker and three journalists.

At around 4:00am on 6 November 1878, they headed off from the
Beechworth railway station into the Woolshed Valley. Recent rains made
the journey treacherous, but their first stop was the Sherritt selection,
which they immediately surrounded. A small detachment of a dozen, led
by Nicolson and Sadleir, attempted to find the Kellys and their as-yet

unnamed accomplices in an outbuilding. Sadleir's horse refused to jump over the fence, so while he broke the fence down Nicolson shouldered open the door to the building.

In the excitement, Constable Bracken tried to rush in, but Nicolson shoved him aside causing his gun to discharge, those outside immediately assuming they were being shot at. This prompted the assembly to close in on the house as Sadleir entered. The room turned out to be the bedroom for the Sherritt children, which the police soon realised was annoyingly devoid of any bushrangers. When John Sherritt was interviewed, he provided no useful information.

The next stop was Aaron's selection nearby. When they arrived, it was empty and had been for days. The report on the incident published in *The Argus* described the arrival at Aaron's home:

"Upon entering this hut young Sherritt was not found, and from the appearance of the squalid den, the sole furniture of which consisted of a large bunk, a rough table, and stool, it was evident that neither the proprietor nor any of his acquaintances had been there that night."

Having no luck there, the police charged further afield to the Byrne selection. At this time dawn had not yet broken and the small army of troopers and volunteers briefly camped at the selection. Though Joe had not been formally identified as a member of the gang, his description had prompted someone to suggest the first mystery man in the gang was a "Bob Burns". The alleged involvement of the Sherritts seemed to conform suspicions enough for police to direct their attention to the Byrnes of the Woolshed Valley.

Margret Byrne emerged from her homestead with her children,

initially quite frightened by the huge number of men and horses that had just come thundering up from Sheepstation Creek without explanation, but once she discovered that she was not in trouble her demeanour changed considerably. Mrs. Byrne was known to be prickly, and this was no exception. Sadleir believed that he could convince her to hand her son over to the police for his involvement with the outrage, which had not at that time been confirmed, in exchange for leniency with his sentence. Mrs. Byrne's response was the blunt and uncompromising, "He [has] made his own bed, let him lie on it."

No doubt Mrs. Byrne's reluctance to outright implicate her son in the murder case, or to turn him in, must have been frustrating for the police.

It was just before dawn that Senior-Constable Strachan brought Superintendent Sadleir's attention to the arrival of Aaron Sherritt, explaining that he would know what was going on as he was a known associate of the Kellys.

Sadleir naturally assumed authority over interviewing Sherritt, who he had never met before. When Sadleir attempted to wrangle a deal, Aaron was unconvinced at his capacity to deliver. Sadleir suggested Nicolson, but again Sherritt was unconvinced that the Assistant-Commissioner had the seniority to deliver what he wanted. Finally, Captain Standish was brought in and engaged in a parley. A verbal agreement was met wherein Joe Byrne's life would be almost certainly spared if Aaron Sherritt could convince him to turn in the other three members of the gang. Superintendent Sadleir would recall to the 1881 Royal Commission:

> "When you come to talk to a criminal, you have to put things wrapt up according to their disposition. Some men you may speak plainly with. Sherritt said always he would have nothing to do with Joe Byrne, and I think we said we will save Joe Byrne; we will guarantee to save Joe Byrne. That was the promise that he wanted,

and he was not satisfied with my authority. Then I called the other officers one by one, and he was at last satisfied. His bargain was if we would save Joe Byrne and guarantee his life, and Captain Standish said, "No doubt the Government would set upon his recommendation in the matter." That was about the size of what was said. [...] It was proposed that he should have an understanding that Captain Standish would recommend to the Government that Joe Byrne's life should be saved, not his liberty, and that he should be tempted through Aaron Sherritt to lead the police on to the other three."

No doubt, at the conclusion of the discussion both men came away feeling like they had somehow gotten one over on the other. Sherritt and Standish were gambling men, however while Standish's vice was horses and he was assured in his ability to back a winner, Sherritt was more of a poker player, and he was keeping his cards close to his chest. We will never know if Standish truly intended to follow through on his recommendation as per the agreement should Byrne turn traitor as arranged, nor if the government would have even accepted his recommendation if he had submitted it.

Superintendent Nicolson was not at all appreciative of Standish's decision to make deals with informants out in the open. Nicolson was one of Victoria's first detectives and as such had developed some very successful strategies for building networks of spies to keep him informed on the movements of his prey. The key to the success of such a scheme however is secrecy, which is not something that can be achieved by making deals out in the open. As far as Nicolson was concerned, the arrangement with Sherritt was doomed to fail, though he appreciated that Sherritt was exactly the sort of man the police needed to help them catch the outlaws.

For Sherritt's part, we can only guess at what his true motivations were when making his deal with Standish. On the surface it looks merely to be a case of Aaron making a special arrangement to protect his best mate from the gallows, even if it is at the expense of three of his other associates. Perhaps it indicates where Aaron's allegiances had been all along – that regardless of the repeated trouble he led Joe into it was never done with an intention to get him into trouble, and that, at the end of the day, one Joe Byrne meant more to Aaron Sherritt than all the Ned Kellys the world could throw at him.

It could also be speculated that Aaron never intended to follow through on his end of the bargain, that it was merely a bluff designed to see where the police stood. It is interesting to note that at this stage the only agreement that was made was simply that if Ned Kelly, Dan Kelly and the third, then-unknown member of the gang were to be turned in by Joe Byrne, an effort would be made to prevent his execution. There was no talk of money or of Sherritt giving the police information. In fact, under the agreement, Aaron's entire role was to convince Joe Byrne to turn on his mates.

By the time the deal had been struck, the small army was disbanding and slowly dispersing, and the Byrne children were mingling with the remaining men quite unaware of their purpose in being there. Margret Byrne was keeping an eye on Aaron Sherritt, however. It seemed that once again Joe was up to his neck in trouble and Aaron was characteristically unconcerned. The difference was that this time it wasn't a matter of a stolen cow having been killed, it was a matter of cops having been killed. Regardless of the repercussions for Joe, the repercussions for the family had the potential to be equally as devastating, or worse.

8

Hare's Hope

The Kelly Gang had struck fear into the colony of Victoria and the police were desperate to find any useful leads possible to get on their trail. New legislation, called the Felons Apprehension Act, was passed enabling the government to declare the gang outlaws. This meant that the protections of the law no longer applied to them and as a result they could be shot on sight without challenge and there were no negative repercussions for their killer. In addition, harbourers could land in gaol for fifteen years if found guilty of rendering assistance to the outlaws. Moreover, the government had incentivised killing the gang by offering a reward of £2000, which was an incredible sum to the average farmer living in Kelly Country. Yet despite this nobody was either able or willing to sell the outlaws out and in early December the gang reappeared near Violet Town to begin the next phase of their career.

On 9 December they stuck up Younghusband's station at Faithfulls Creek to use as a base of operations while they robbed a bank in Euroa the following day. It was an audacious plan and though many bush-rangers had attempted bank robbery very few had succeeded. Even the legendary Johnny Gilbert and John O'Meally had resoundingly failed when attempting a bank robbery, but Ned Kelly was determined to find the money he needed to pay off his harbourers.

Ned rode into the station and called in at the homestead asking for the manager, Macauley. One of the servants, Mrs. Fitzgerald, was per-forming her chores and informed Ned that Macauley would be out until the afternoon. Her husband was having lunch in the kitchen and asked who the visitor was. Ned replied by asking who Fitzgerald thought he was. "You could be Ned Kelly for all I know," came the response and Ned was only too happy to let him know how good at guessing he was.

Joe, Dan, and Steve had all arrived by this time and assisted their leader in rounding up the male staff and locking them up in a storeroom. The gang's horses were stabled, fed and groomed and the prisoners kept under armed guard.

That evening a hawker named James Gloster arrived at the station to camp the night. It was common practice for travelling salesmen to camp at farms along their travel route, and Gloster was well acquainted with Younghusband's station. He was bailed up by Ned and Dan as he attempted to get some water and though he offered resistance, with Ned flying into a rage when he saw Gloster make a move for what he assumed was a pistol concealed behind the bench of the wagon, the hawker was soon subdued. Gloster and his teenaged assistant Becroft were added to the number in the storeroom before the gang raided the hawker's wagon. They stole clothes, boots, and perfume in order to spruce themselves up. Their ragged bush clothes were then discarded and burnt.

That night Ned allowed himself to be openly questioned by his cap-tives and happily answered any questions they had about what happened with Fitzpatrick and at Stringybark Creek. Meanwhile, Joe put the finishing touches to a letter that Ned wanted to have delivered to Donald Cameron, a member of Parliament who had used the outlaws to make a political point, seemingly showing interest in the apparent misconduct of the police. Ned had mistaken this for sympathy and believed that if he sent this politician a letter giving his side of things, Cameron could potentially be a powerful ally. Joe also played concertina for Mrs. Fitzgerald, demonstrating that no matter the situation he always made time for the fairer sex and music where possible.

The following day Ned, Joe and Steve knocked down the telegraph poles near the train station, which was a short walk from Younghusband's, then mangled and cut the wires in order to prevent news getting out about their presence. Ned and Joe then bailed up a party of kangaroo hunters who mistook them for plainclothes police. The hunters were relieved of their conveyance and weaponry then locked in the storeroom with everyone else.

After lunchtime Ned led a convoy to Euroa, leaving Joe on his own to guard the prisoners in the storeroom. Joe patrolled the area around the storeroom with a rifle in each hand and at one stage was overheard seemingly talking to a man named Jack. An effort by Fitzgerald to hack through the wall to freedom with an axe was stymied by the other prisoners who feared that if the other outlaws found Joe dead, they would seek revenge on the captives.

In the early afternoon a train passed through, and a line repairer disembarked to find out what had happened to the telegraph. With a handful of cut wires, he made his way across to Younghusband's station on foot hoping to find answers. Instead, he was bailed up and imprisoned by Joe.

Meanwhile the rest of the gang had arrived in Euroa and were setting about their ambitious task. There were very few people in town as there was a funeral taking place for a local boy named Bill Gouge who had been killed in a riding accident, and most of the townsfolk were in attendance or preparing to attend. The bank was also conveniently out of view of the local police.

Dan guarded the rear of the bank where the manager's family resided, while Ned went to the front with a cheque, demanding to be let in to cash it. When the clerk opened the door to tell him to leave as they were closed for the day, Ned forced his way in and bailed up the staff. He was joined by Steve, who had locked the manager's family up in the house on his way through the building, and together they emptied the cash drawers. Ned demanded access to the safe, but the accountant only had one of the keys, the other was with the bank manager Robert Scott.

Scott was found in his office attending to book-keeping when Ned and Steve burst in and ordered him to hand over the key. After much back-and-forth it was revealed that the key was somewhere in the house at the rear. Ned went to the house and sought out Scott's wife who then found the key in the study and handed it over. Ned cleaned out the safe and then announced that Scott, his staff, and his family would have to come back to Younghusband's station with them. Due to the size of Scott's family the gang took possession of his buggy in addition to the hunters' cart and hawker's wagon that the gang had already used in the ride up.

When the convoy returned, the new arrivals were permitted to mingle with the other prisoners. Ned once again spoke to his captives, but this time gave the instruction that nobody was to leave until three hours after the gang had departed. Joe, having finished Ned's letter to Cameron, asked Mrs. Fitzgerald for postage stamps to put on the envelope. The letter would be sent some time after the gang had left.

The outlaws did not leave until after nightfall and when they did, they performed some daring horseback vaults over the fences and then split up to make it harder for the police to track them. Most prisoners did not abide by the time limit Ned had set down, though none made an effort to report the events until the following day. The Kelly Gang had cleared out with around £1500, which would soon fall into the hands of their sympathisers.

In consequence of the robbery, the reward for the gang was raised to £4000. This was equal to the reward offered for Ned and Dan's idol Ben Hall and his gang in 1865, and was an unseemly amount of money that demonstrated the depth of desperation the authorities were in. Still, nobody was willing to shoot them down or turn them in either through fear or sympathy.

Additionally, Joe Byrne and Steve Hart were now officially identified as the two mystery men, meaning that from now on they would have to be far more careful about their movements.

Though it was never proven, it is more than likely that Aaron Sherritt received a payout from the robbery. He had been living life the way most of the Kelly sympathisers had been – hand to mouth. Residing in his "squalid den" on a block of land he could not afford to keep up payments on, described in his lease application as "totally unfit for cultivation – being only fit for grazing paddock", Aaron eked out a living grazing cattle and breaking horses but barely keeping his nose above the water line. He was constantly in trouble over his rental arrears, and it wasn't until after the Euroa robbery that he mysteriously found the money to catch up.

Shortly after the Euroa affair, Superintendent Nicolson was suffering from fatigue and an eye infection and Standish took him off the Kelly hunt. In his place he put Superintendent Francis Augustus Hare, one of the most senior policemen in Victoria. He and Nicolson had worked together in 1870 to capture the bushranger Harry Power and Standish considered that this experience placed Hare favourably to be able to catch the Kellys.

On 31 January 1879, Aaron made a trip into Benalla and attempted to speak to Captain Standish at the police station. He was informed by Hare that Standish was out of town for the evening. Aaron stated that he wished to speak to Standish about something important, and after some back-and-forward revealed he had information about the Kelly Gang. As Hare described the event:

"I led Aaron to believe I did not care to hear his news, but kept him engaged in conversation. I had heard his name and knew who he was. Captain Standish informed me, when he returned, that he had never seen him either from the day he spoke to him at that Sebastopol affair, at Mrs. Byrne's. [...]
Sometime after — about an hour — Sherritt said, "I think I can trust you with my information;" and then he told me that on the previous afternoon, about two o'clock, Joe Byrne and Dan Kelly came to his selection. This is not Mrs. Sherritt's house; Aaron was not at that time living with his mother, he was living on his own selection; it was mid-way between Mrs Sherritt's and Mrs. Byrne's. He said Joe Byrne came to him whilst he was working on his selection. He told me Joe Byrne jumped off his horse, and that he had always been his most intimate acquaintance; he said he came and sat down beside him; he had been his schoolfellow and with him in crime nearly all their lives; he said Dan Kelly was very suspicious, and would not get off his horse, and did not get near him, and he said they sat talking for a long time, and then asked him to join them, as they were going across Murray, and intended going

to Goulburn, in New South Wales, where the Kellys had a cousin. He said they urged him to go for a long time as a scout. Sherritt never told me that at that time they were going to stick up a bank. He told me he refused to go with them, and after some pressing, Joe Byrne said, "Well, Aaron, you are perfectly right; why should you get yourself into this trouble and mix yourself up with us." He said they were talking to him for about half an hour, but kept looking round and watching every move that was made. [...] He was a remarkable looking man. If he walked down Collins street, everybody would have stared at him — his walk, his appearance, and everything else were remarkable. I said, "Be careful, now you are in Benalla, that you are not seen here; do not go into the town, but get some hotel near the railway station"; and I gave him £2 for coming down to give this information."

If this had been a deliberate attempt to lay bait to draw the police away from where the outlaws were to cross into New South Wales, then Hare took it hook, line and sinker. He even got Aaron to describe Ned's and Joe's horses and draw their brands for him so that police could identify their mounts; Ned's preferred horse was a bay mare with white hind legs named Mirth and branded with an E conjoined with a reversed K, Byrne's horse was a grey mare named Music, and the Byrne brand was a B in a circle.

Hare felt confident, and in the days following that fateful meeting some of the information Sherritt had provided seemed to corroborate with details being reported to police by witnesses that had seen some of the gang in that time. Unfortunately for the police the gang were not going to Goulburn at all, but Jerilderie which is around 450km further west.

On 7 February 1879, the Kelly Gang crossed the border, briefly visiting the Woolpack Inn on their way to Jerilderie to gather information about the township and its law enforcement from the barmaid, Mary Jordan, *alias* Mary the Larrikin. The following night they instigated their audacious plan by rousing the local police, Senior-Constable George Devine, and Constable Henry Richards, from their beds and locked them up in the logs. The outlaws took up residency in the police station, which doubled as the family home for Devine and his wife and children and established it as their headquarters for the weekend.

The next day they took turns to disguise themselves in the troopers' uniforms and pretend to be police reinforcements sent to protect the town against themselves, while in fact they were patrolling the town to get a good layout of it in preparation for their grand finale. Dan Kelly took Mrs. Devine to the local courthouse to monitor her as she prepared the space for that day's mass as the town had no designated church. When they returned, Ned and Steve dressed in uniforms and escorted Richards around the town.

Jerilderie's main drag was small, and its noteworthy buildings were conveniently close together. These included the telegraph office, blacksmith, newspaper editor's office and most importantly the hub of the town – the Royal Mail Hotel and Bank of New South Wales. The bank and the pub were conveniently conjoined by a short passageway, which proved very useful for the gang's plans.

Most of Sunday night was spent compiling the information that the gang had gathered, including a photolithograph of the layout of the township they had acquired, in order to more efficiently map out their plan for the next day.

Inspired by the famous raids performed by the infamous Gilbert-Hall Gang in the early 1860s, and likely also by the raids by the Clarke Gang of the nearby Braidwood district in the middle of that same decade, the plan was to round up the entire town and keep them prisoner in the pub while they robbed the bank. Further to this, the telegraph was to be destroyed to prevent news leaving the town just like at Younghusband's Station, and Ned was to have a letter printed by the newspaper editor.

Having failed in his bid to have Donald Cameron use his previous letter to begin the process of freeing Ellen Kelly and instigating reforms of the police force, Ned felt the only way to see justice done was to make his own point of view publicly known. The letter was little more than a rewrite of the previous one but expanded to include more information about what he felt was evidence of police corruption and persecution against him and his family, as well as more threats towards his enemies. Once again, Joe was employed as the scribe and his more lyrical and whimsical flourishes are dotted throughout the letter, softening Ned's frequently violent proselytising and braggadocio. In later years it would come to be referred to as the "Jerilderie Letter" and held up as an important piece of Australian literature.

One notion that Ned seemed keen to drive home in the text was the penance for betrayal. Loyalty was one of Ned's core values and naturally he felt that it was desirous that disloyal persons ought to be punished severely. He stated:

> "...any person aiding, or harbouring, or assisting the police in any way whatever; or employing any person whom they know to be a detective, or cad; or those who would be so depraved as to take blood money, will be outlawed and declared unfit to be allowed human burial. Their property either consumed or confiscated, and them and theirs and all belonging to them exterminated of the face of the earth. The enemy I cannot catch myself I shall give a payable reward for."

Clearly, anyone Ned Kelly found to be a traitor was in for a world of pain and retribution.

After finishing the plans and writing the last remaining bits of Ned's letter, Joe felt free to indulge himself in his favourite things: consuming alcohol and spending time in the company of women. According to contemporary reports, Joe rode back to the Woolpack Inn and spent a considerable amount of time drinking and being entertained by Mary the Larrikin before leaving in such a sozzled state that he had to be helped into the saddle. It is unlikely that Ned would have been impressed by this.

On the fateful day, Monday 9 February, the gang kicked everything into gear. In the morning Joe took the gang's horses to be shod at the blacksmith's – all charged to the government account of course – before accompanying Dan to investigate the town's telegraph system. Next, Constable Richards was escorted to the hotel by Ned and Dan, with Joe and Steve riding close behind. Richards introduced the Kelly brothers to Cox the publican and the gang set up shop inside. As patrons entered, they were taken prisoner by Dan in the bar or Joe and Steve in the front room. Other locals were herded like sheep into the pub by Ned to be kept under armed guard, while also being plied with drinks that were to be paid for by the gang in order to keep them quiet and cooperative.

When the gang were satisfied that the preparations were completed, Joe passed through the corridor that joined the pub to the bank and stuck up the bank staff by presenting a pistol and proclaiming, "I am Kelly; bail up!"
Ned and Steve soon joined him, and the till was emptied. As it only contained £700, Ned rapidly became indignant and asserted that there must have been at least £10,000 in the bank. The accountant, Edwin Living, was hesitant to comply with the gang's demands and tried to stall things,

at first stating that there was no more money to be had. Ned discovered a hidden treasure drawer that required a manager's key to open. It was beginning to look like a repeat of Euroa.

Joe was more lateral thinking than Ned, and rather than relive the rigmarole from the first bank robbery he had a far simpler solution: smash the thing open with a sledgehammer. This was overruled and it emerged that the bank manager, Tarleton, had just returned from a trip out of town and he was taking a bath. The key was located, and Steve was left to guard the manager as he finished washing himself and dressing. When Tarleton finally emerged, he was dressed in a silk coat and smoking cap.

Meanwhile the local schoolteacher, William Elliot, had wandered into the bank and was bailed up by Joe Byrne. Upon learning the identity of the new captive, Ned sent Elliot back to the school to send his students home, declaring a holiday in honour of the gang's visit. Ned had also located the bank's records and began grabbing as many as he could with the intention of destroying them. He was under the belief, as misguided as it was, that by destroying the bank's records of its debtors it would relieve the strain on poor farmers. Living was permitted to retrieve his life insurance policy, but the rest were taken to be burned.

The bank robbery was again interrupted, this time by a trio of men consisting of the postmaster, his assistant, and the newspaper editor, who, upon realising what was transpiring, bolted. The outlaws captured two of the men but the one that got away was the man Ned wanted most – Samuel Gill, the newspaper editor. Gill kept running until he was well outside the town, which would see him later ridiculed in the press as a coward. Along with Gill disappeared Ned's hopes for getting his letter published, or so he thought. He eventually ended up entrusting the fifty-plus pages to Edwin Living to be forwarded to Gill for printing.

As was proving to be a recurring theme, Ned's trust was misplaced and Living handed the letter over to the authorities instead.

The prisoners were marched back through to the pub whereupon a disagreement erupted between the hotel's Chinese cook and Joe Byrne. The Chinese man refused to comply with directions to go into the bar and when the obstinate man continued to refuse the orders, pretending not to understand what he was being told, Joe clouted him across the head. This seemed to instil an immediate compliance. Joe then rode to the telegraph office and ordered the destruction of the Morse key while examining the records of that day's missives, before re-joining the others at the hotel.

Ned once again took the opportunity to address his captive audience with a long lecture detailing the various grievances leading up to the shootings at Stringybark Creek. The raid proved to be a great success for the gang and went off considerably more smoothly than their previous effort. As the gang left town, a bundle of loot was placed on Joe's saddle and Dan and Steve rode up and down the main street waving revolvers around and shouting, "Hurrah, for the good old days of Morgan and Ben Hall!"

When the gang split up upon leaving the town, Ned and Steve paired up while Joe went with Dan. Ned and Steve headed to the Traveller's Rest Hotel. There Steve stole a saddle to replace his own, then bailed up Reverend Gribble and took his watch. Gribble went to Ned and expressed his distaste for Steve's behaviour. Ned responded by publicly berating Steve and forcing him to return the watch. Steve complied but it was unclear whether Ned was more annoyed at the act of petty theft, the complaint from Gribble, or the fact that the watch was far less valuable that what Steve had already taken that day. Ned had another drink, conspicuously placing his revolver on the counter and announcing that anyone looking for the reward on his head could come and grab it and shoot him if they had the intestinal fortitude. There were no takers. Ned left the bar with yet another threat, this time stating that if anyone were to raise an alarm then Jerilderie would be awash in its own blood.

In the end, the gang got away with close to £2000, all of which soon made its way into the hands of their sympathisers. Joe made sure his family and best mate were given the lion's share of his cut of the loot. Margret Byrne was able to pay off her debts and go on a shopping spree, and Aaron Sherritt allegedly received £250 from Joe.

It is impossible to say exactly how much money Joe handed out to people in the Woolshed from the robbery as the bills were unmarked and therefore untraceable. This meant that if any sympathisers made purchases using the stolen money it would be impossible for police or bankers to determine if the notes had come from the bank at Jerilderie. It was a bit of good fortune for the gang and their supporters.

In response to the outrage, Sir Henry Parkes, the premier of New South Wales, entered into an agreement with the Victorian government and a consortium of banks and the reward of £4000 was doubled. The actions of the gang were a major affront to the New South Wales government and law enforcement, especially given that the bushranging plague that had afflicted the colony in the 1850s and 60s had been effectively suppressed by that point. The audacity of the gang was enough to make the New South Wales police force crack down on bushranging with incredible resolve and a heavy hand.

By the time Victorian troopers had reached Goulburn news of the gang's audacious raid of Jerilderie was already being telegraphed throughout the colonies. Hare immediately set up guards along the Murray to try and prevent a crossing, but it was to no avail.

Despite the bad information in relation to the gang's New South Wales expedition, Hare took a liking to Sherritt and maintained his

90

services, even if his colleague Sadleir openly disapproved. Something had convinced Hare that Sherritt's intentions were honest, and he believed that his closeness to Byrne gave him an edge over the other police spies.

With this in mind, Hare arranged for Aaron to meet him in Beechworth with Detective Ward. After a detailed discussion, Aaron suggested that the gang would probably stop at the Byrne selection for supper on their way back from Jerilderie. Plans were immediately made by Hare to meet Aaron that evening in the vicinity of El Dorado so that he could direct the police to where the gang would be. When Hare asked Ward his opinion the detective, with years of experience dealing with Aaron and Joe Byrne, was said to have replied, "I have known Sherritt for years, and if he likes he can put you in the position to capture the Kellys, but I doubt his doing so."

Nevertheless, at 8:00pm Hare and Ward arrived at the meeting place where Aaron was waiting for them. After a considerable time, it became apparent that the party of police from El Dorado was not going to show up and the trio set off without them. Aaron led the two officers through rough terrain until he spotted a fire in the distance. Hare ordered Sherritt to go and investigate. Aaron took off his boots and wandered into the bush making barely a sound. When he returned, he informed Hare and Ward that the fire was several miles away. He took them into the bush and led them onto a precipice where he then pointed out a campfire burning on a ledge in the distance. The decision was then made to head straight to the Byrne selection.

When they arrived, Aaron scoped the place out and directed their attention to a candle burning in the window that he claimed was a signal for the outlaws. The trio remained hidden in the scrub watching the Byrne stockyard until morning. It was, of course, fruitless. If the gang really had intended to swing past and visit Joe's mum, they either had changed their minds or had visited and left before the arrival of Sherritt, Hare and Ward.

Aaron was probably surprised that Hare had stuck with it and pressed his luck further by suggesting they set up a police party in the mountains that overlooked the Byrne house. He recommended that during the day they could sleep in the same cave where only months earlier he had guarded the gang as they attempted to evade police in the wake of the Stringybark Creek tragedy, coming down at night to watch the stock-yard where the gang would surely put their horses. Aaron neglected to mention that from such a vantage point it severely limited their ability to see the whole selection, thus creating blind spots where the gang or any members thereof, could potentially slip in unnoticed. This didn't seem to bother Hare, who immediately formed a party of "picked men" for the task.

Night after night, Aaron would accompany the party as they staked out the Byrne property. In the evening he would visit his sweetheart Kate, pumping her for information, or at least this is what Hare presumed he was doing with her. When he left the house, he would join the police and give any updates he had gotten during his visit. He maintained that this was the place the gang were most likely to visit, and if not the whole gang, at least Joe Byrne.

Hare soon learned exactly what sort of person Aaron Sherritt was, declaring, "He was a splendid man, tall, strong, hardy, but a most out-rageous scoundrel."
Nothing entrenched this reality more than an incident wherein Sherritt had secretly convinced one of the constables in the party to help him steal the Jerilderie booty from the bushrangers when they arrived at the Byrne selection, which they would then split between themselves.

At this time a party of native police from Queensland led by Sub-Inspector Stanhope O'Connor was sent to assist in tracking the gang down. While Hare mostly concerned himself with the cave party that was assigned to watch the Byrne property, O'Connor was out in the field with Sadleir following leads. Despite not having direct contact with Sherritt at the time, O'Connor was soon made aware of the El Dorado larrikin by reputation.

In March of 1879 Aaron received a letter from Joe Byrne written in coded language. Likely the phraseology was that which the young men had developed in those far more carefree days stealing horses from squatters, intended to obscure incriminating messages. Aaron said to the police that in the letter Joe was asking him to meet him at Whorouly races where he intended to get Aaron to ride a black mare in one of the hurdle races for him. Though the letter was deemed legitimate by the handwriting, the notion that Aaron at nearly six feet tall and of sturdy build was an appropriate choice of jockey did not ring true. The assumption was that Aaron had deliberately obscured the message. Regardless, men were put on duty at the races in disguise in case the outlaws did indeed show up. They did not.

It seemed that Aaron had cast something of a spell over Hare, who would remember him fondly thereafter. Even when addressing the Royal Commission years later, Hare could not help highlighting exactly how remarkable Aaron was, and in so doing explain how formidable a challenge it was to catch men of such calibre as Ned Kelly:

"Aaron Sherritt's knowledge of the movements of the police was wonderful. He said he was the scout, or head-centre, of the district; that he could give me any information about the movements of my men in any part of the district. I said, "I do not believe you." He said, "You may question me — try me if you like — and see if I do not." So, I asked him one day, "Can you tell me what has occurred the last few days, or the day before yesterday?" He said, "Yes; Detective Ward and other men rode out of Beechworth, a party of police have come into El Dorado, and some men through near Everton; but I do not know the particulars beyond that there are some policemen there." I said, "Now, Aaron, will you tell me how you got to know?" He said, "I will not." I said, "Why; are you not in my confidence?" He said, "No; there are certain things I will not tell; I will tell nothing against myself to convict me, although I have been in all the crimes with the Kellys for years past." It would take me a week to tell the half he said. All this time this man was faithful and true to me. I say he was a man of most wonderful endurance. He would go night after night without sleep in the coldest nights in winter. He would be under a tree without a particle of blanket of any sort in his shirt sleeves whilst my men were all lying wrapped in furs in the middle of winter. This is an instance that occurred actually: I saw the man one night when the water was frozen in the creeks and I was frozen to death nearly. I came down and said, "Where is Aaron Sherritt?" and I saw a white thing lying under a tree, and there was Aaron without his coat. The men were covered up with all kinds of coats and furs, and waterproof coatings, and everything else, and this man was lying on the ground uncovered. I said, "You are mad, Aaron, lying there"; and he said, "I do not care about coats." [...] He was born on these mountains. I said to him on one occasion, "Can the outlaws endure as you are doing." He said, "Ned Kelly would beat me into fits." He said, "I can beat all the others; I am a better man than Joe Byrne, and I am a better man than Dan Kelly, and I am a better man than Steve Hart. I can lick those two youngsters to fits; I have always beaten Joe, but I look upon Ned Kelly as an extraordinary man; there is no man in the world like him, he is superhuman." Frequently, when he has been lying by me at night, he said, "You will catch Joe, Steve, and the others," and I said, "Why," and he said, "He is too —— smart." I said, "If he comes here, I will get him." He said, "No, except you take great caution; do you think that Ned ever goes in front? No, he sends the other three a hundred yards ahead." I said why do they obey him, and do that; and he said, "He carries out his orders at the point of his pistol." I said, "This must come to an end"; he said, "No; I look upon him as invulnerable, you can do nothing with him," and that was the opinion of all his agents; nearly everyone in the district thought him invincible. When the police had a row with any of the sympathisers, they would always finish off by saying, "I will tell Ned about you; he will make it hot for you some day," never speaking about the others at all."

When Aaron wasn't sneaking into the police camp for a spot of breakfast, he was usually found at his selection or at his parents' place. At night he would happily carry supplies for the police and camp out with them. He would tirelessly stay up all night with Hare, regaling him with stories of the exploits of his life, including the criminal activities he had engaged in with Joe Byrne and Ned Kelly.

Hare began to call him "Tommy" in public as Aaron was too uncommon a name and would be easily recognised. Despite Hare's continued faith in Aaron, the other police continued to have misgivings.

If Aaron's endgame was to get the Kelly Gang captured, he was doing an awful job of it as no progress had been made in his time working with the police. Rather, it seemed that he had slowed down their progress by about a month. It was as if his entire purpose was to keep the police looking exactly where the gang weren't.

If so, then all the misgivings held by senior officers like Sadleir and Ward, as well as the majority of the lower ranking men in the party, were completely justified. Yet, Hare was convinced he was genuine in his desire to help the police. At this point Aaron was still not receiving a wage for his involvement with the police, he was volunteering, but if he was short of money Hare would loan him a pound or two where appropriate.

With months passing and no sign of the outlaws being apprehended, the mania around the Kellys was reaching fever pitch. Captain Standish had begun encouraging police to arrest suspected sympathisers and keep them on remand as long as possible until there was enough evidence to lay charges under the Felons Apprehension Act. It was hoped this would starve the gang out of hiding. This meant there were families throughout the Kelly Country that suddenly lost breadwinners for an indefinite period of time on the suspicion that they were helping the outlaws. Yet somehow the gang continued to remain at large, unchanged.

Some considered that the act of locking men up on suspicion of being harbourers with no intention of ever releasing them would only embolden the outlaws and the remaining sympathisers who remained at large. Fortunately for the men in question, Magistrate William Henry Foster, who had been overseeing the process of remanding the prisoners while police tried to gather evidence against them, finally made the executive decision to give the men their liberty. He deemed it unjustified to extend the remand and ten sympathisers were freed on 25 April 1879.

If suspicious eyes had been cast in Aaron Sherritt's direction, wondering how he had avoided police scrutiny unlike so many other known associates of the outlaws, he clearly took no notice.

9

Mrs. Byrne Smells a Rat

Complications arose on the twentieth day of the stake out when Margret Byrne on one of her many wanders around the selection spotted a strange man carrying a bucket to the creek. It was one of the men from the party stationed in Joe and Aaron's old hideout. On further investigation she located a block of soap, footprints, and wood shavings from where a policeman had been whittling a stick in order to pass the time. She immediately confided her concern to Aaron that there were police watching the house and implored him to scout the area for her to see if her supposition was correct. Aaron told her not to worry and he would take care of it. He pretended to ride around looking for police the next day, but Margret was unconvinced and began to view Aaron with suspicion.

Two days later Margret's suspicions hit paydirt. Alerted by the sun glinting off a discarded sardine tin, she crawled up into the rocks and saw Sherritt asleep with his hat over his face along with several police.

The sentry quickly noticed Mrs. Byrne retreating and roused Hare. When Hare woke Aaron to announce that he had been spotted, Aaron went white as a sheet and declared that he was a dead man. Hare gave Aaron his coat and helmet as a disguise and told him to make his presence known elsewhere in the district to provide an alibi, which the startled Sherritt did immediately.

That evening Aaron returned to the selection and got Mrs. Byrne's attention by playing a flute outside of her house. He was admitted inside where a discussion was had. When Aaron joined the police that night for his watch there was good news and bad news.

"She has lost her faith in me, but she did not recognise me. She said, 'A pretty fellow you are, going to search; I found the men in the mountains to-day.' [...] I am all right; I am still on terms of intimacy with the others in the house."

Mrs. Byrne had also intimated that she had only seen one man that morning but knew from the way the area was beaten up that there must have been many more and would be happy for Joe to shoot fifteen or twenty of them.

The following day Margret Byrne once again went crawling amongst the rocks but this time the police saw her coming and a constable was sent to scare her off. While she was crawling around a boulder, the constable pounced on her. She screamed, "What! What! I am only looking for cattle. I will get my son to shoot the whole bloody lot of you."

Hare only remained with the parties for another few days before cutting his losses and returning to Benalla. He left the parties in place for a fortnight before they too withdrew. Aaron had been adamant that he was the way to get to the gang, and that he was in communication with them. While Margret's faith in Aaron's fidelity to her family was shaken, so to was Hare's faith in Sherritt's capacity to bring the gang into the waiting hands of the police.

Soon after this, the engagement between Aaron and Kate Byrne was called off. It was clear that he no longer had the trust of the Byrnes, but he still seemed to have support from the outlaws —at least for the time being.

10

Charlie the Horse

The dust had barely settled after the engagement was broken before Aaron was making moves on Kate Kelly. It is unknown to what degree Aaron was already familiar to the Kelly sisters, but it hardly comes as a surprise that sixteen-year-old Kate would have caught Aaron's eye. Though he was much older that her, it was not uncommon for girls at the time to be married at sixteen or younger, and usually to older men. Despite his attempts to woo young Kate, he was rebuffed. This coincided with controversy over a horse named Charlie.

While still an item, Aaron had gifted a filly to Kate Byrne but had told her that if she didn't intend on keeping it then he would take it back to sell. Whether on Kate's or Margret Byrne's instructions, Paddy Byrne, Joe's younger brother, sold the filly to a Chinese man and received a gelding in the exchange.

Margret Byrne subsequently accosted Aaron about horses he had grazing on his selection that she believed were police horses. Aaron denied the claim and having no evidence to the contrary Margret simply informed Aaron that if he had knowingly been grazing police horses, she would burn his house down.

Aaron, fuming over the sale of the filly as well as Mrs. Byrne's tirade, stole Paddy Byrne's gelding, which had been named "Charlie", seeing it as compensation for the filly. Aaron then sold the horse to Kate Kelly's sister Maggie, who was unaware it was stolen, though she had her suspicions.

Margret Byrne filed charges at the end of May and a warrant was issued for Aaron's arrest. It was alleged that Margret had offered to drop the charges if Aaron would leave the colony. Clearly Aaron's response was in the negative.

Just after the charges were laid the gang paid a visit to the Sherritt family selection and took Aaron droving with them. It is very possible that they had heard the news of Aaron's falling out with Mrs. Byrne and wanted to test his loyalty. It was not the only instance of the full gang testing the validity of such accusations.

On 26 June, Joe Byrne wrote a letter to Aaron requesting a meeting, referring to the concerning allegations made by Ned and Dan's relatives that he was railing against:

> *Dear Aaron I write these few stolen lines to you to let you know that I am still living I am not the least afraid of being captured dear Aaron meet me you and Jack this side of Puzzel ranges Neddie and I has come to the conclusion to get you to join us I was advised to turn traitor but I said that I would die at Neds side first Dear Aaron it is best for you to join us Aaron a short live and a jolly one the Lloyds and Quinns wants you shot but I say no you are on our side If it is no thing only for that sake of your mother and sisters We sent that bloody Hart to your place*

twice did my mother tell you the message that I left for you I slept at home three days on the 24 of may did Patsy give you the booty I left for you I intend to pay old sandy doig and old Mullane Oh that bloody snob where is he I will make a targate of him meet me on next Thursday you and Jack and we will have another bank quite handy I told Hart to call last Thursday evening I wold like to know If he obeyed us or not if not we will shoot him if you come on our tracks, close your puss you know you were at Kates several times you had just gone one night as we came we followed you four miles but returned without success If you do not meet me when I ask you meet me under london you know. I will riddle that bloody Mullane, If I catch him no more from the enforced outlaw till I see yourself

    I remain your truly

You know

On 2 July Aaron and Ward discussed the proposed meeting and Ward encouraged Aaron to keep the appointment. The detective then sent a letter to Hare announcing as much. When Aaron reported back to Ward, he stated that he had gone to the meeting point, but Joe Byrne had not appeared. Seemingly he had not taken Jack with him, as stipulated by Joe, either out of choice or because Jack was unavailable, though it seems unlikely that Jack would have given up the opportunity to get information about Byrne to report back to the police.

Given that Joe had specified two different locations where they could meet it is clear he considered the meeting as one of great importance. It is unlikely that if Aaron attended the appointment in the correct location that Joe would not have showed up. So, if Aaron did meet Joe and then reported otherwise to Ward it must have been a lie. Was Aaron attempting to throw the police off Joe's scent? Had he agreed to deliberately misinform Detective Ward to prove his loyalty to his mate and in turn the gang? It would be reasonable to suggest as much.

Knowing what the Lloyds and Quinns were saying about him behind his back must have been a heavy burden on Aaron's mind. It is impossible to know what Joe took away from the meeting if it did indeed take place, but he may not have been completely convinced that Aaron and his family were all on the same page, or indeed that they were all working to help preserve the gang. There were more tests to come.

Regardless of what the outlaws made of him at the time there was still a warrant out for Aaron's arrest, and he decided he wasn't willing to face court and potentially end up in the clink, so went into hiding, mostly laying low at his father's place.

Two police from El Dorado who had been keeping an eye on the Sherritt selection arrested Jack Sherritt as he opened the door early one morning, taking him out in handcuffs. The whole time Jack protested that it was a case of mistaken identity. When eventually he convinced the troopers to take him to Crawford's selection nearby, while *en route* to the El Dorado lock up, the mistake was made plain, and the police had no option but to release their prisoner and return to the selection on Sheepstation Creek. Naturally, by the time they got back Aaron had done a runner. The rumour was that Joe Byrne was with him at the time.

Aaron was now living as a fugitive himself, and wrote a note to Jack that gives a small insight into his frame of mind at the time:

> *I want if you please half pound to baco their is £5 reward for my whereabout but the party told him not for that manny hundred I am afraid he will some night walk home with with out his horse saddle and bridle I have my bloody eye on him I intend to take him prisoner myself and lock him up*

This scrawled letter with its lack of proper spelling and grammar was addressed to "M Sheck" of Flagstaff, which was probably a code name for Jack. The "he" referred to is most likely Paddy Byrne. After all, it was because of Paddy's horse that Mrs. Byrne laid the charges leading to Aaron's brief spot of bushranging. There seems to be an indication that Aaron intended to take Paddy prisoner if he could ever catch him walking without a horse to escape on. He also refers to the "party", which likely means the police cave party, with whom Aaron was presumably still in contact. It does seem curious that he should remain in contact with police with a warrant for his arrest active.

Aaron was finally arrested on 14 July and taken to Beechworth. For the first time in years, he was forced to endure the unpleasantness of being locked up in the holding cells with forgers and public nuisances. The next day at the Beechworth Police Court, Inspector Brooke-Smith requested Aaron be remanded for seven days while the case for the prosecution was built and witnesses sought. Bail was granted and set at £50 or two payments of £25, and for once Aaron was able to pay it. After Aaron's arrest, Detective Ward was visited by Jack Sherritt who intimated that on the night of the arrest he had snuck up to the Byrne homestead to eavesdrop. He claimed that, with Aaron nabbed, Joe Byrne would pay his mother a visit. Like much of Jack's hot tips this did not bear any fruit.

On the 22nd, Aaron Sherritt's committal hearing took place in the Beechworth courthouse before two hundred people who were hoping to get a glimpse of some of the notorious identities connected to the Kelly saga. The crowds left disappointed, however, as Sherritt's defence counsel had been delayed *en route* from Albury.
Aaron was remanded to stand trial the following Saturday, his bail enlarged accordingly.

Finally, on 26 July Aaron stood trial for horse stealing before William Henry Foster. Among the witnesses were Ellen Byron, the former sweetheart of Joe Byrne, Maggie Skillion and Paddy Byrne. When Margret Byrne took the stand, her approach was to deny everything that had been said against her including her threat to burn Aaron's house down, the suggestion that Aaron and Kate Byrne had been engaged, and that Aaron had stayed with her for any length of time (both Ellen Byron and Paddy Byrne had stated that Aaron frequently stayed at the Byrne house for extended periods, Ellen even suggesting he had lived there around three of four years.) It was not a good look as her evidence did not corroborate with that of the other witnesses. A notable absence was Kate Byrne. It can only be guessed at as to why her evidence was either not sought or not offered, not that it would have likely altered the outcome.

The case was complicated but there was not compelling enough evidence to suggest that Aaron had violated any contract by taking possession of Charlie the horse as compensation for the filly. There seemed to be a lot of questions around what justification Margret had in lodging the charges in the first place, especially given it was not her horse that was taken, nor was it an agreement made with her that had supposedly been violated. The charges were dropped, and Aaron walked free, but the damage was well and truly done. Now the Byrnes' suspicion of Aaron was mingled with a feeling of resentment about the case not going their way, and they believed that the police had somehow interfered in the case to get Aaron off. Margret Byrne would later suggest to Enoch Downes, a truant officer that had visited her about her son Denny not attending school, that she considered Aaron getting off to be a "dodge" on the part of Detective Ward, designed to incite the outlaws into the open. Indeed, it was her assertion that Ward was constantly trying to find ways to incite Joe to seek revenge against Aaron.

At this time there was another notable spy reporting to Ward after watching the Byrne selection — none other than Ah On. It seems that the bad blood over the incident in 1877 remained, and for one reason or another Ah On was inclined to let the police know when his neighbour's infamous son was popping in for a visit.

In a memo that Ward sent to Assistant Commissioner Nicolson, he stated:

"He is unable to describe the Colour of the Horses his name is Ah Onu [sic] he was Complainant in a Case where Joe Byrns [sic] and Aaron Sherritt assaulted him, Senr. Constable Mullane being the arresting Constable, at the time and has no doubt that Ah Onu could not be mistaken as to the identification of Joe Byrns, as he has lived for years within two hundred yards of Mrs. Byrns house."

As much as the Byrnes wanted to peg Aaron as a fizgig, there were clearly far more threats to contend with and some were closer to home than they had noticed.

THE KELLY GANG: PORTRAIT OF AARON SHERRITT.

An etching of Aaron Sherritt based on a contemporary studio portrait.
The original photograph upon which the likeness is based has long since
vanished.

*Source: The Australasian Sketcher, July 17, 1880. [Courtesy: State Library Victoria;
A/S17/07/80/164]*

PORTRAIT OF BYRNE.

Joe Byrne - an etching based on post-mortem photography.
Source: The Australasian Sketcher, July 17, 1880. [Courtesy: State Library Victoria;
A/S17/07/80/168]

A studio portrait of Aaron Sherritt taken by James Bray, Beechworth.

[Courtesy: Burke Museum, Beechworth; 10237]

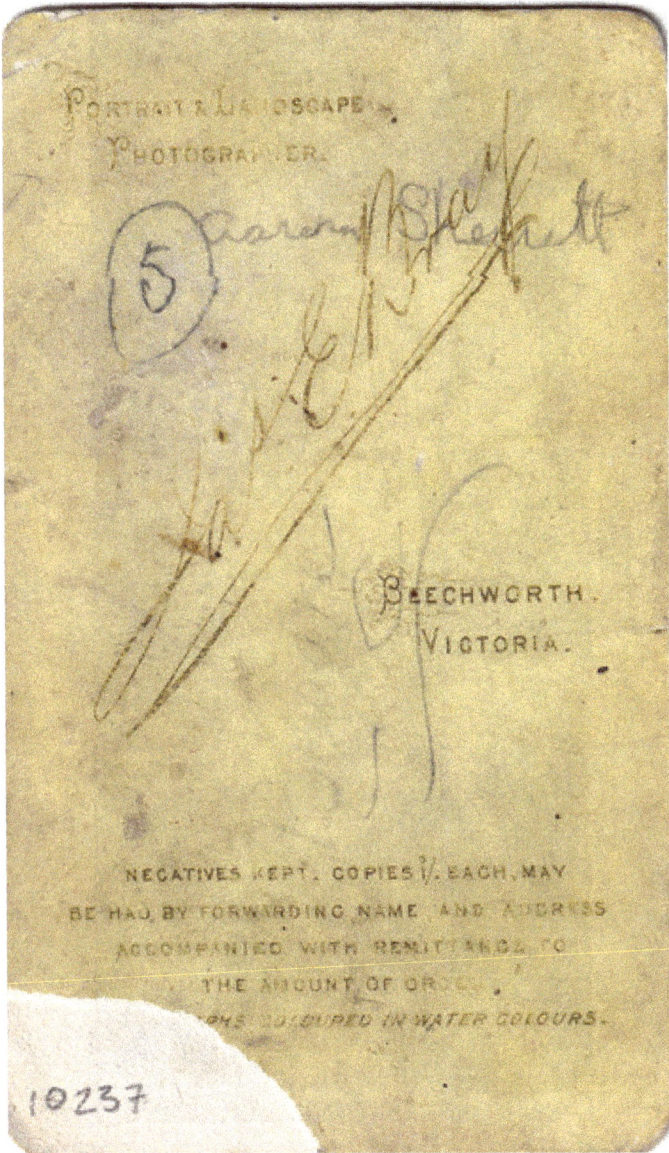

The reverse of the Bray 'carte de visite' features, among many notations, the faint, underlined inscription from its previous owner, "Beware" (center, vertical).

Aaron Sherritt in a lost Bray studio photograph. It is possible this was taken as a wedding portrait, but was later used by press artists as the basis for their illustrations after his murder. This version was featured in a posthumous newspaper article.

Source: The Sun, 05 September 1911

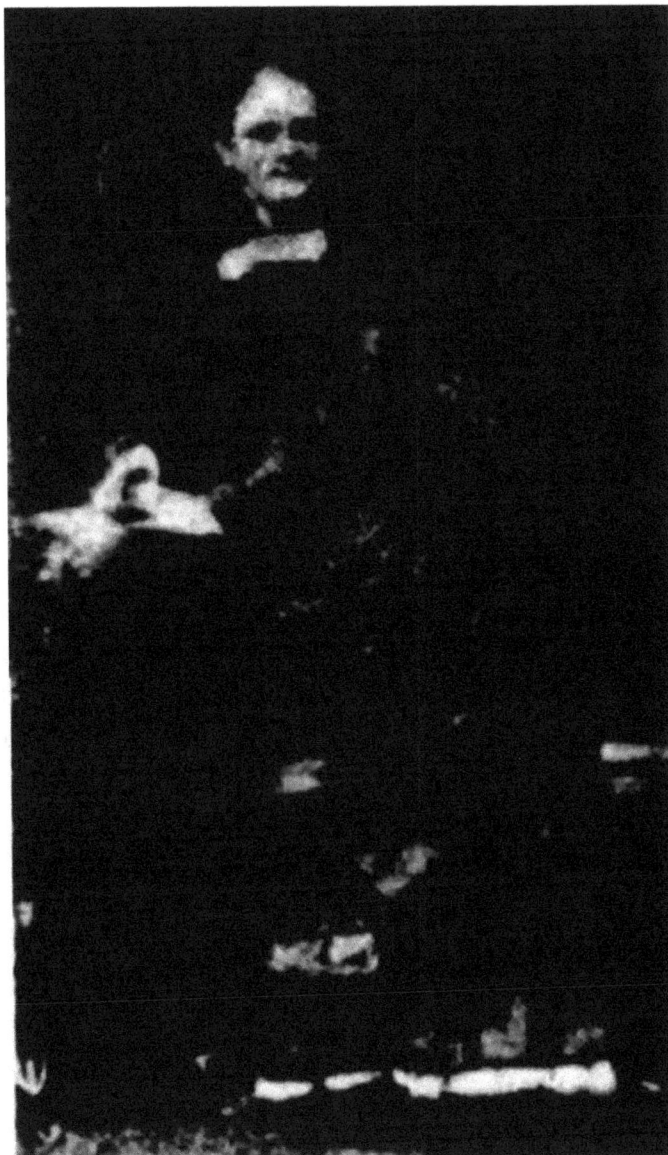

Ellen "Belle" Sherritt (née Barry) photographed in Bray's studio circa
1879. This may have been taken as a wedding portrait at the same time
as the one of Aaron.

Source: *Register News Pictorial, 11 May 1929*

11

Double-Agents

In the middle of the horse stealing saga, Superintendent Hare had taken ill, having injured his back, and been replaced by Nicolson, who was brought back from Melbourne for the job. One of his first actions as head of the investigation was to secure Aaron Sherritt on a wage to act as a spy rather than the flimsy verbal agreement he was previously bound by. If Sherritt really was worth his salt, then he could prove it by fully dedicating himself to the police cause. Nicolson was determined that if he was going to be in charge then things had to be done his way. Of course, this did not sit well with Standish, who sent word to Nicolson to cease to employ Sherritt, considering him an untrustworthy character. Nicolson was adamant that Sherritt was key to closing the net on the Kellys and began to pay Sherritt out of his own pocket to ensure he was getting compensated for working with the police. He would later be re-imbursed, but for Nicolson, who had complete faith in his methodology, it was a matter of principle above all else.

Another of Nicolson's initiatives upon taking the reins was to properly establish, in December of 1879, a permanent party in the caves around the Byrne selection. This party would consist of two parties of four men alternating to watch the Byrne selection at night after sleeping in a cave during the day. Assigned to the task were constables Robert Alexander, Newman Hagger, Henry Armstrong, Daniel Barry, James Cox, Alfred John Falkiner, Robert McHugh and James Dixon.

As part of his arrangement with Nicolson, Sherritt was required to accompany the police on their night watch duties. The police remained sceptical of Aaron, refusing to believe he could ever turn on his mates. The proverbial leopard does not change its spots, after all. It was also decided that a new codename for Aaron was necessary. Ditching Hare's "Tommy", Aaron was now known officially as "Moses", the brother of the biblical Aaron's namesake.

In fact, Nicolson was keen to ensure that all his informants were given a level of protection by being given codenames. Amongst the roster of police spies were Aaron's old mentor in crime John Phelan, who was to be referred to as "Paddy", and Paddy Allen, a Beechworth storekeeper who knew the Sherritts and Byrnes well, who was to be referred to as "Allingham".

Detective Ward also became more heavily involved at this point and made arrangements with the aforementioned Paddy Allen, to provide supplies for the police. As often as was required, Allen would load the supplies for the police in his cart along with his other deliveries and during the day would deliver the goods to the Sherritt selection, from whence Aaron would take them to the police camp. Every day Aaron was tasked with carrying water to the camp in bags, and occasionally his brother Jack would help him carry bags of tinned food to the police.

Allen would, in this period, become something of a confidante to Aaron, who would visit the storekeeper with information to be forwarded on to Detective Ward. Aaron refused in many cases to see Ward personally about the information as he feared what the sympathisers would do if they saw him talking to the detective. Frequently he would report sightings of one or more of the outlaws around the Byrne selection, but never in a manner that the police could utilise.

Decades later, Allen would be interviewed by a journalist named Brian Cookson about the days of the Kelly outbreak and he would reflect fondly on the kind of person Aaron Sherritt was:

> "Sherritt was a man who would do anything — all was the same to him, so that it paid. I used to have a pair of big knee boots that he badly wanted to get. I told him I had an execution out against a man at the Woolshed, and that if he'd run in enough of the man's cattle to satisfy the judgement the boots were his. He did it, at once."

The so-called cave party's routine was established by Nicolson, Ward and Mullane and required the men to camp in the caves about the Byrne selection then emerge at 10:00pm to spy on the house. Evidently the unofficial directive regarding Joe Byrne as per Aaron's agreement with Standish remained in play, as Constable Henry Armstrong, who was part of the party, would later testify that they were told by Nicolson that, "Should the outlaws go to Byrne's, let you all fire on the tall man; that will be Ned, and then you will have so many boys to deal with. But should Byrne come alone, take him alive if possible, convey him to Beechworth by night; or if you cannot convey him by night, keep him all day until the following night. That is with a view of using him to assist in the capture of the three remaining outlaws."

This deal seems to have been well known as Paddy Allen would later recall that it even got so far as the reaching Joe Byrne. Joe's reputed response was, "No; I'm in it, and I'll stick to it!"

If true, it would have been incredibly frustrating for Aaron who had been working hard to get the police on his side to ensure that a deal could be brokered in the first place. Apparently, Joe had now completely shifted his allegiance from his boyhood companion to the most wanted man in Australia. For Aaron it must have felt something like betrayal.

When the cave party went out on their nightly stake-out of the Byrne selection, Aaron was required to accompany them, but he was to be positioned lower down the slope in the long grass. They would maintain watch until daybreak when they were to break up the camp, clean up any litter and clear away any traces of their presence such as footprints. Aaron's duties were to make sure the men left in time and ensure no traces were left behind.

From the outset, Standish made it clear to Nicolson that he did not approve of the party and repeatedly ordered it to be disbanded. It is unclear how much of this was a genuine concern about the secrecy of the operation and how much was fuelled by Standish's well-known animosity towards his colleague.

There are many anecdotes that give an insight into the strangely juvenile behaviour of some of the police at this time. Just one of the cases of such behaviour concerned a trooper assigned to the cave party named James Dixon. He had heard rumours about Aaron's toughness and goaded him into a fight. As Paddy Allen would later recount, Dixon drew attention to comments Aaron had supposedly made about being able to lick any man in the police force. Aaron in his usual cocky way replied, "I can lick you anyway."

True to his word, Aaron gave the trooper a belting and as Dixon ran off towards Beechworth to report Aaron for assault, blood all over his white shirt, Anne Sherritt intercepted him on a bridge. The matriarch calmly reminded Dixon of Ward's orders and the possibility of a sacking if Ward discovered they had been disobeyed. Dixon returned to the camp where a mock trial was held and subsequently Dixon's colleagues strapped him to a bed and force fed him a case of porter until the entirety was drunk.

Nicolson sent orders via Detective Ward for Jack Sherritt to meet him in Wangaratta around the time the cave party was being formed in order to recruit him as a police spy. Jack said that he needed time to think about it and three weeks later met Nicolson again in Beechworth and agreed to help the police. Jack was given the codename "Jones" and assigned duties under Constable Alexander, and as the police work was so demanding on his time, he was forced to give up his employment fencing the Crawfords' selection.

Jack explained to Nicolson that the outlaws frequented Mrs. Byrne's selection, thus reinforcing Aaron's assertions and subsequently Nicolson's faith in their ability to help the police catch the outlaws. Though Jack would later publicly claim he informed Nicolson about the gang's presence at the Byrne selection after Jerilderie and Nicolson refused to take action, it is unlikely given that Nicolson was no longer in charge of the case at that point, nor had the cave party been established yet.

Another incident that soured Jack's attitude towards the police came following a night drinking with Paddy Byrne. While Paddy knocked back spirits, Jack kept to the "soft stuff" to stay sober for the purposes of interrogating young Byrne. He would claim that Paddy told him, "Joe has been home and got some clothes, and cleared out; is not he a bloody smart fellow?"

This was not the only time that Jack had heard that Joe would receive supplies, especially laundry, from his family during nocturnal visits. Jack filed the information away and the following morning encountered two of the cave party returning to the camp after fetching water. He informed them that he had been told that Joe Byrne had been at the selection getting clothes the night before. The information was dismissed. Jack then went into Beechworth and informed Detective Ward. The next time that Jack met with the cave party the police sneered and mocked him, asking him sarcastically, "Did you see Byrne last night?"

Jack would claim that after his information was ignored several times by Nicolson and Ward, he went back to working for Crawford, but Nicolson soon organised to meet him at Paddy Allen's store. Here the wily, old Scotchman paid Jack £5 in £1 notes and promised him that if he continued to work with the police, he would gain the biggest portion of the reward money. This seemed to do the trick, and Jack would afterwards go above and beyond to report every sighting and divulge details of conversations he had with Joe Byrne. He was determined to get his hands on a slice of the £8000 and there was no sense of there being any form of loyalty to Joe Byrne or any of the rest of the gang for that matter, though he would maintain the appearance of having sympathies with them for the purpose of potentially luring them into a situation where they could be captured.

Evidently, the doubts about the fidelity of the Sherritts was still a concern and weighing heavily upon Joe Byrne. On 28 August Aaron received a threatening letter from Joe, the details of which are now lost to time. It was reported to the police but once again the information amounted to nothing. By now Joe's behaviour was becoming somewhat erratic and his fear about the trustworthiness of Aaron and Jack was becoming something of an obsession as he continued to test them.

At the beginning of September Joe Byrne tasked Jack with publicly posting a letter and caricatures he had penned in Beechworth. After Jack received the letter from his sister, he handed it in to Detective Ward who immediately leaked the letter to the press. These were subsequently described in the *Ovens and Murray Advertiser*:

"Detective M. E. Ward, at present in charge of this district, and who is universally and deservedly respected as a most zealous officer, received a threatening letter, bearing the Beechworth post-mark and purporting to have been written by a member of the Kelly gang of outlaws. The writer of the letter (which is now in the hands of the Chief Commissioner of Police) threatens to murder Ward at the first opportunity which offers itself, and concludes by warning him to prepare for his "latter end." The police are using every effort to discover the author of the missive; and that they may be successful is the earnest wish of every respectable member of the community."

There was a large tree at the corner of the outside of the Beechworth post office that was used as a community notice board where the threatening letter was allegedly posted by Detective Ward himself. Ward's objective in publicising the threats against him is unclear, though perhaps it was an attempt to illicit sympathy or incite further outrage among the Beechworth locals against Byrne and his bushranging cohort. Jack believed that the gang were unaware that he had not followed the instructions, or at least trusted him enough not to pry, but it is very likely that they were already suspicious.

On 6 September, Aaron once again met with Joe Byrne. He would not report it to Nicolson until ten days after the fact and, even then, he would not provide any useful information about the meeting. It is tantalising to think that this was Joe extending an olive branch to his mate after months of niggling doubts, but it seems unlikely.

On 19 September, Joe visited his mother's house and left £2 in silver for Jack Sherritt as payment for delivering the threatening letter. The money would be conveyed to Jack via Paddy Byrne. If Joe still had doubts about the Sherritts he was not letting on.

The process of gathering information was not an easy one for the police and while Nicolson and Sadleir were wrangling often erroneous or unserviceable reports in Benalla, Ward was doing his level best to act as spymaster in Beechworth with the Sherritts as his main agents as they seemed to provide the most consistently reliable information. No doubt his experience with Aaron and Joe in the past led him to believe that the pair were very unlikely to have remained apart, even with Joe facing the death penalty and a reward of £2000 on his head. Every one of the family members was always listening for information or covertly performing tasks for the police. The entire family, according to Paddy Allen, was in the employ of the police, evidenced by the government cheques he was given to hand over to them as payment for their services rendered.

Detective Ward had recruited Anne Jane Sherritt to monitor the area between the Sherritt and Byrne selections. Ward referred to her as, "a secret, cunning, good girl."

The Sherritt matriarch was also making a point of gathering information and frequently forwarded letters to Ward, usually written by herself, relaying information given to her by her children.

An example of the sheer, baffling complexity of the acquisition of information is illustrated in the following anecdote imparted by Ward:

"On one occasion Ann [sic] Jane Sherritt said she received a letter from Mrs. Byrne to go and see her, and Mrs. Byrne told her then that Joe Byrne and Dan Kelly called at the Black Dog Creek. Joe Byrne gave a letter to Mrs. Byron to deliver it to Mrs. Byrne. Mrs. Byron, not being on good terms with Mrs. Byrne, she sent the letter by her husband to Batchelor, who lives next door to Byrne, which he delivered to Mrs. Byrne. We had enquiries made, and found that Byron was at Batchelor's just about the time, and that is how I proved her [Anne Jane] to be true to me."

Another of Ward and Nicolson's key agents early on was James Wallace, Aaron and Joe's schoolmate. Wallace was working as the school-master at the half-time schools at Hurdle Creek and Bobinawarrah, as well as the local postmaster, when he had heard of the police murders and wrote to Captain Standish in December of 1878 to offer his ser-vices in collecting information. Standish declined, however in July 1879 Nicolson met with Wallace and discussed the possibility of utilising him as part of the network of police spies. Wallace claimed that he was in indirect contact with the outlaws through mutual acquaintances, citing communication between himself and Byrne regarding a saddle that Ned Kelly allegedly stole from him some time prior. Who was Wallace's inter-mediary? None other than Aaron Sherritt. This coupled with Wallace's good social standing as a schoolmaster seemed to be good enough reasons for Nicolson to engage his services and the arrangement agreed upon was that Wallace would, in his spare time, do his best to gather informa-tion from Kelly sympathisers in exchange for remuneration of expenses incurred in the process. And just as with the other spies, Nicolson gave him a codename — Wallace was to be known as "Bruce", likely a little in-joke by the Scotsman (William Wallace and Robert the Bruce being national heroes in his homeland).

Like Jack Sherritt, James Wallace held no steadfast allegiance and would readily impart information about the outlaws where he found it, and if he ended up throwing Aaron under the wheels in the process it did not seem to concern him. Indeed, his relationship to the Sherritts was a rocky one already, having previously stolen and slaughtered one of Jack Sherritt's cows.

He had taken some of Jack's cows into his paddock, claiming that he had no animals to keep the grass in check. When Jack came to collect the animals, one was missing. Wallace claimed it had died but it soon emerged that he had killed it, butchered it and divided the carcass amongst his family. He subsequently instructed Jack not to say anything to his father about it. Thus, as much as Wallace likely assumed a degree of intimacy with the Sherritts there was good reason for them to be on their guard around him.

Wallace was constantly keeping tabs on the movements of the Byrnes and Sherritts, and reporting back to Ward, then eventually Nicolson directly when he grew to dislike Ward. Though he was not receiving a regular payment for his information, the expenses he was asking reimbursement for were raising eyebrows. They were usually related to horse feed and alcohol, as he supposedly had to drink with sympathisers to loosen their lips and then had to ride over long distances to Benalla to give information to Nicolson. By his own account these expenses would amount to £80 in the time that he assisted police, though the police would state the amount he actually claimed was £180.

One of James Wallace's favourite games was to pump Jack Sherritt for information whenever they would cross paths. Jack grew suspicious of the questioning and on one occasion when asked whether he had seen any police about, Jack responded that he had seen several troopers along the road. Two hours later Margret Byrne had already received the news and had expressed her opinions of it to one of the Sherritt girls, probably Anne Jane, as she passed by the Byrne selection. What Wallace did not know is that it was a test; there had been no police on the road at all. This seemed to confirm Jack's mistrust of Wallace, and highlighted the fact that Wallace was placing an arbitrage bet on the outcome of the pursuit; anticipating making a profit regardless of whether the outlaws were caught or not.

It was hardly the first time, nor would it be the last time, that Wallace would relay information from the Sherritts to the Byrnes. On another occasion he briefly stopped at the Sherritt selection at Sheepstation Creek where he saw Aaron resting on the floor. He went straight to Margret Byrne and told her that Aaron and Detective Ward were having tea at the Sherritt place.

Through it all, Wallace maintained a pretence of fraternity with Aaron Sherritt, who spoke openly with him about a great many things regarding his involvement with the outlaws and police. It was during one of Wallace's frequent visits to Sherritt's hut that Aaron let slip that the gang typically moved from camp to camp within a fifteen-mile radius of Greta, focusing on the regions around the King River, Sebastopol and Warby Ranges. Yet, despite this information later proving to be quite accurate, it was never followed up by police in such a way as to result in a capture.

Wallace also dabbled in "mesmerism", an antiquated pseudoscience popularised by Franz Mesmer in the 18th century, also referred to as "animal magnetism". The term originally pertained to Mesmer's utilisation of the healing powers of magnetism on energies within the body, sometimes literally treated with magnets. Over time it more broadly referred to the practice of inducing a hypnotic state using body movements such as stroking and waving, similar to what is performed in Reiki in the present day. James Wallace would practice mesmerism on Aaron

Sherritt, presumably hoping that in a hypnotic state Sherritt would be more susceptible to imparting information. Though he would gain no useful information this way, and quickly abandoned it as a method to extract information from Sherritt, Wallace would later brag about the influence he had over Aaron.

Not long after the Jerilderie affair, he took bank notes from Aaron to be cashed at Wertheim's in Beechworth, and upon discovering it was likely a note from the Jerilderie robbery he made sure to cash it in Detective Ward's presence. He later expressed dismay that no action had been followed up by the detective.
Wallace believed that Ward was a bungler whose incompetence was frustrating the pursuit of the outlaws, and thus he attempted to convey his information directly to Superintendent Nicolson in person where possible, stating in one letter that, "there is a screw loose in your department somewhere."

Over time Wallace would even come to believe that Ward was plotting against him in order that he should capture the Kelly Gang on his own without the assistance of the spies. This was seemingly reinforced by an incident in September of 1879 that Wallace was supposedly informed of, wherein Ward announced to a group of people at a ploughing competition that Wallace was supplying information to the police about the outlaws. Wallace would claim that this is why many sympathisers he had been gathering information from began to be guarded around him, including the Sherritts and Byrnes. According to James Wallace, this was followed by Ward placing him on a "black list" of informants to avoid, which in turn somehow instilled a sense of camaraderie between himself, Jack Sherritt and Paddy Byrne. As he wrote in a letter dated 26 November 1879:

"Rode down through the Woolshed, [...] Met John Sherritt, junior, and Pat Byrne (Joe's brother). I had a long and interesting conversation with these worthies, who manifested much pleasure in meeting me. I wondered at the marked change in Jack's manner towards me, as, on two or three previous occasions, he had carefully avoided me. I soon ascertained the reason. It appears, by their account, that the virtuous detective who is standing the season at Beechworth had stated, a day or two previously, that my 'name had been added to the black list at the office; that he believed that bloody Wallace was in constant communication with the outlaws.'"

Wallace's detestation of Ward was something of an obsession, and he readily perpetuated (or more than likely instigated) a rumour that Ward had seduced Kate Byrne. He seemed determined to publicly besmirch Ward at any opportunity, which did nothing to endear him to the police who were already growing tired of his useless information of dubious origin and were increasingly suspicious of him potentially being a double agent. When Nicolson eventually warned Jack Sherritt to watch what he said around Wallace, it was yesterday's news.

Wallace had already become aware that sympathisers not only knew the movements and activity of the police but were actively feeding the information back to the outlaws. Specifically, Wallace held the belief that it was Aaron and Jack Sherritt that were feeding this information to the gang, acting as double agents themselves in order to trick the police into a false sense of security while gathering the information for their mates. It never seemed to occur to him that hypocrisy was not a good look when trying to appear virtuous.

One of the assertions that Wallace made to Nicolson was that he knew where Sergeant Kennedy's watch, or "chronometer" as he called it, was. He divulged that Aaron had told him that he had the watch and was investigating ways to remove stains from it, which Wallace suggested meant he was looking for a way to remove the inscription. According to Jack Sherritt, however, neither himself nor Aaron had ever been in possession of the watch. Indeed, Jack had heard James Wallace offering to pay Mrs. Byrne if she would arrange to have the watch forwarded to from Joe Byrne. When this move failed to hit paydirt he tried to bribe Aaron to make a statement that he had the watch and then ask for the watch from Mrs. Byrne. This produced no result. Unsurprisingly, when Wallace convinced Aaron to ask the same from Kate Kelly, this also had no positive result.

Kennedy's watch would eventually be returned by an anonymous intermediary to the dead sergeant's widow long after the events of the Kelly outbreak had settled into collective memory. Perhaps if any watches taken from the dead police were in Aaron's possession it was Lonigan's, given to him by Joe Byrne after Ned had demanded he have it returned to Lonigan's widow. Ned was known to carry Kennedy's watch, and Dan had given Scanlan's watch to Becroft, the hawker's assistant, at Euroa. Given that Joe was known to wear rings stolen from Scanlan's and Lonigan's dead bodies, it is likely that he was in possession of Lonigan's watch. It is important to note that although Wallace asserted that Aaron had Kennedy's watch, he could never attest to having actually seen the watch in Aaron's possession. If Jack's claims were true this is a perfect illustration of the way in which James Wallace had tried to manipulate Aaron for his own purposes, as well as evidence of the unreliability of the "information" provided by the schoolmaster.

As the Kelly hunt continued without the police seemingly coming any closer to their target, and with said police being told to keep their distance from James Wallace, the spurned schoolmaster began to write hit pieces for the Wangaratta Despatch criticising the police effort, disguised as a romantic serial called *Christmas in Kelly Land*. Evidently, Wallace considered himself something of a wordsmith and would claim that when pumping the Byrnes and Sherritts for information it was in service of a novel he was writing. When asked later what happened to the notes he made, he claimed he had destroyed them all.

In the end, Nicolson grew tired both of Wallace's infuriatingly delayed reporting — some updates coming three or four weeks after the fact — as well as his useless or likely false information and refused to further engage with him. This seemed to push Wallace over the edge, and he began launching ever more scathing attacks on the police where possible, including a verbose and dense letter sent to James Howlin Graves, the member for Delatite, in April 1880. In the letter he rips through Nicolson and Ward, as well as ridiculing the Queensland native police and the overall police pursuit. He also had choice words to say about Aaron Sherritt and his ilk:

"In my opinion, those men that are hired at a high salary should be dispensed with. If Aaron Sherritt or any of his class ever intended to sell the Kellys, they would have done so long ago for the £8,000, and the department would not be the laughing-stock of the outlaws and their sympathizers. Fancy a man in his proper senses engaging Aaron Sherritt to sell the outlaws. Why he would rather cut his arm off. The fact of it is Ned Kelly's best friends are engaged by the department, and why are they engaged is the question. If there are not men in the force capable of doing any duty that is required of them, the whole force should be disbanded. Are the trackers required? If they are not, they ought to be sent to Coranderrk, and it would save the country £130 a month at the very least, and the sub-inspector could return to Queensland, as he is never troubled with the trackers. Is Detective Ward and the Assistant-Commissioner capable of outwitting the outlaws? My answer is they are not. What they have done up to the present time is nothing, and I believe they will continue doing nothing, and the Kellys will reign until they die a natural death."

12

Fraying at the Seams

In October of 1879 Aaron began courting Ellen Barry, better known as Belle, who had been working as a servant for James Ingram. Belle was a fifteen-year-old whose mother, also named Ellen, was well known in the district due to her work as a midwife. Her father, Ned Barry, was a miner but also infamous in certain quarters for his involvement with stock theft. The Barrys were Roman Catholics and when Aaron proposed to Belle this caused significant friction between him and his own family. His mother in particular was so incensed by the suggestion that Aaron would not only marry outside of the family's Anglican faith, but convert to Catholicism to facilitate it, that she essentially disowned him and a period of direct antagonism towards Aaron from his family members began. The only member of the family that seemingly refused to keep step with the rest was Aaron's younger brother Willie, who managed to somehow disregard the politics and remained close with his brother.

Jack Sherritt would later downplay the antagonism, stating that he and Aaron had merely been at odds for a couple of days because he feared that if Belle's siblings were mingling with the Byrne siblings at school it could compromise the efforts of the cave party. His actions would not back up such an innocuous stance.

It was the opinion of Belle and her mother that the rift was not actually about religion. Aaron has stated to Belle that he identified as "nothing", thus whether he was a Protestant or Catholic was irrelevant. Rather, it was their belief that the conflict came from the fact that Aaron would no longer be providing his father with free labour.

As evidenced by the incident with the wounded horse prior, John Sherritt seemed to consider that his sons had something of an obligation to work for him. The idea that Aaron would assert his independence must have rankled the old man severely. After all, this was a man that was more worried about losing money because of a load of hay getting wet, than the son who he had ordered to sell it being thrown in gaol for animal abuse when caught using a horse that he himself had allowed to become injured from damaged equipment.

Perhaps John felt that Aaron owed him labour as repayment for all the times that he had swooped in to help pay the rent on Aaron's selection? John was not exactly rolling in money himself, so it would not be out of the question for him to hold that over his eldest son's head as a way of strong-arming him into doing chores. No doubt this put a heavy strain on Aaron's relationship with his family, and this might also explain why he gravitated to the more welcoming Barrys.

At the end of October, Joe Byrne corresponded with the Sherritts through several letters. Every one of them was shown to the police who encouraged the Sherritts to fulfil the requests as much as possible to inspire confidence, and hopefully lure Byrne out of hiding so they could capture him. Joe had concurrently decided to test Jack Sherritt's loyalty, and he wrote to him, conveying the letter through Anne Jane Sherritt, requesting a meeting at a farm at Sandy Creek belonging to a man named Thompson, a former boundary rider from Peechelba Station. Naturally Jack went straight to Superintendent Nicolson with the letter, and Nicolson instructed him to keep the appointment as it could provide the perfect set-up to capture the outlaws. Jack did as was requested and rode out on the appointed date to the abandoned farm on 6 November.

Much to Jack's disappointment, Joe did not show up and Jack camped the night. The following morning as he began to return home Joe emerged from the bush and signalled for Jack to join him. Joe presented a dreadful sight to Jack, clearly having ridden his horse harder than was reasonable, likely out of a sense of urgency. He would recount the scene later to the Royal Commission:

> "He asked me if I knew Mr. Hare, and I said "No"; and he said, "That is the old buck that caught Power." I said, "I do not know." He said he believed he was a smart old "cove"; and he asked me if I knew Mr. Nicolson, and I told him I knew no one; and I was to go to Yackandandah and see how many police were stationed there, and to let him know, [...] and see if I could detect any police in private clothes, and loaf round there and see where the police went in to have tea, and all particulars about their movements. [...] He had no horse, but he had a pair of long boots, and his trousers were all over blood. He had long spurs. I asked where his mates were, and he said, "Not very far off." [...] I was to meet him at Evans's Gap a short time afterwards."

During the conversation Joe also discussed how Hare's party had almost caught up to the gang several times and that the outlaws were "bloody well starved out." He promised Jack that once they knocked over the bank, he would give Jack one or two hundred pounds. It is interesting to note that Joe also expressed to Jack that his mind was particularly burdened by the murder of Sergeant Kennedy. It was not recounted in any detail but it leaves a hint as to what Joe's own feelings regarding the events at Stringybark Creek were, and raises many questions about his own role in the death of Kennedy.

While it is somewhat assumed that the gang were quite flippant about the three police deaths, this expression of remorse gives a fairly clear indication that, at least on Joe's part, the deaths had exacted a heavy toll on their mental health. Perhaps Joe had been wrestling with the reality that it was merely a quirk of fate that had put him in that position, and it had cost him his freedom and liberty? Perhaps there was a grain of truth to the story Aaron had told Hare about Ned Kelly ordering Joe and Steve Hart to fire into Kennedy's body?

At the conclusion of the meeting Joe planned with Jack to meet him again at Evan's Gap for a follow-up meeting. As Jack left, he was under the impression that the rest of the gang must have been secreted nearby, watching him. Whether or not this was the case was left undetermined as no police were sent out to investigate.

On 13 November, Dan Kelly called in at the Sherritt selection at Sheepstation Creek around dusk requesting to speak with Jack. Anne Sherritt stated that he was not home and would not return until that evening. Dan was not prepared to be fobbed off and entered the house with a pistol in hand, looking for Jack. The concerned matriarch stayed at his side as he moved from room to room. The search was unsuccessful, and Dan stated he would return at 8:00pm before riding away.

Immediately after this visitation, Jack was interrupted by Anne Jane as he was doing some work for the Crawfords. She warned him about

the outlaw's imminent return. He saddled his horse and rode into Beechworth, arriving at the police station at 7:00pm. He notified Nicolson
and Ward of the visit and Dan's planned return. Nicolson told him to
go back and speak to Dan Kelly and gather any information that could
help the police capture the gang. Jack was not prepared to risk it as he
believed he had been spotted by some of the Kelly sympathisers when
entering the police station. Ward gave Jack 10 shillings, and he was told
to ride out to the Woolshed and make his appearance known at a place
called Julien's to create an alibi.

Meanwhile, the rest of the outlaws had returned to the Sherritt selection, but as the signal — a lit candle in the window to signify that Jack
was home — was not visible, they left. By the time Jack returned home
they were gone.

On 23 November Joe Byrne held a clandestine conference at Jack's
hut with Aaron in company as well. The Sherritt dogs barked for around
two hours before Joe made himself known at 8:00pm. He shook hands
with all in attendance and thanked Jack for his work forwarding his
threatening letters to the police. He went on to explain that Dan's visit
on the 13th was to inform Jack that the scheduled meeting at Evan's Gap
had been cancelled. As it turned out this was not the only apparent
change of plans.

Joe explained that the Yackandandah robbery had been called off as it
was too dangerous. The new target was to be a bank in Beechworth, and
he wanted Jack to scope it out for him. Joe also explained that his plan
was separate from Ned's and went on to describe it. Joe explained how
he and Dan, assisted by Aaron and Jack, were to operate under cover
of darkness to bail up the bank manager from his bed and make him
empty out the safe and till for them, under pain of death if he refused. If
a second key to the safe was required from a second person, the robbers
would split up with two remaining with the manager so the others could

bail up the second man. Once again, if there was to be any resistance then there would be bloodshed. It was a considerably different strategy to the gang's previous robberies, which seemed more geared towards providing a platform for Ned Kelly to have some public relations, rather than purely focusing on getting cash with which to fund their sympathisers.

Joe appeared to have lost a considerable amount of weight, and he explained that the police appeared to be getting sick of watching his mother's place and seemed to be fretting about their inability to intercept him. He also spoke about how the gang's horses were bad, though his grey mare Music remained the best of the lot. Joe had arrived on foot to the meeting indicating that either he had made his way out of hiding on foot or he had hidden Music in the bush on the outskirts of the property. Although sympathisers frequently provided fresh horses for the outlaws, allowing their animals to graze in their paddocks until the gang returned the animals, the outlaws retained their own animals as much as possible to prevent their presence at the farms of their sympathisers being noticed. If police saw that someone had the gang's horses grazing in their paddock, there would be trouble. However, as an additional measure to confound police, many sympathisers had taken to riding in a formation of four: three of them riding bays and one riding a grey. This proved to be an effective way of generating bad leads for the police. In fact, Joe's brother Paddy had begun riding a grey mare and dressing like Joe to create confusion.

There was a female in attendance at the meeting, though she was never named in official reports. This would have most likely been Anne Jane Sherritt or one of the other sisters. The female in question put to Joe that if he were to surrender himself and give evidence against the other gang members then he may receive a pardon. Evidently Aaron had made it known to his family what his arrangement with Standish had been. Joe simply replied that if he did so he would be considered worse than Sullivan and be chased out of the country.

Sullivan was a bushranger in New Zealand that had handed himself over to police and gave up his mates in exchange for his own freedom. In the circles within which the Kellys moved Sullivan was clearly viewed with considerable contempt, as Ned Kelly would often refer to him when describing the lowest of the low. It is tempting to consider that Joe's invocation of Sullivan may have been a subtle dig at the Sherritts and their disingenuity.

Aaron seemed keen on Joe's plan and Jack agreed to join Joe if the plan went ahead, but never followed up on the mission to scope out a target for robbery in Beechworth. Joe left at midnight and told the brothers that they would meet again on the 30th. It was the last time that Jack ever saw Joe Byrne alive.

At the conclusion of the meeting Jack predictably rode off to meet with Nicolson and Ward. Nicolson told Jack to ensure he followed through on the arrangement as it could lead the bushrangers into a false sense of security. Jack, however, was terrified at the prospect of being implicated in a bank robbery and potentially being arrested or even shot dead by the police if mistaken for an actual member of the gang. Nicolson suggested that if Jack was so afraid that the outlaws would burst into his home and shoot him, he should take to sleeping in the garden.

To pacify Jack, Nicolson arranged for he and Aaron to have their portraits taken in Bray's photographic studio, Beechworth. In these photos the brothers are dressed in their normal attire, with the elastic chinstraps from their hats under their nose in the larrikin fashion used by Kelly sympathisers as a way of recognising each other. These photographs would be given to police to acquaint them with the appearances of the brothers.

Jack's absolute terror at getting involved in Byrne's bank robbery scheme did nothing to endear him to Nicolson and was just one more mark against his name as far as the superintendent was concerned. Ever after, Nicolson would refer to Jack Sherritt as a coward.

It is interesting to note how Joe's plan resembled the infamous Mount Egerton bank robbery years earlier, attributed to the notorious Andrew George Scott, *alias* Captain Moonlite.

In fact, earlier that year, Scott, fresh out of Pentridge, abandoned his attempted lecture tour on prison reform due to police harassment. Subsequently, a bank robbery in Lancefield that August, which was at first attributed to the Kelly Gang, was quickly pinned on Scott and his companion James Nesbitt when the police could not find supporting evidence that the Kellys were responsible. In reality it was neither the Kellys or Moonlite, but two men named Samuel Lowe and Christopher Bray.

Following this harassment, Scott had become a bushranger and began heading into New South Wales with Nesbitt, Thomas Williams, Thomas Rogan and Gus Wernicke. At the same time as Joe Byrne and Dan Kelly were testing the loyalty of the Sherritt brothers, Scott and his mates had been trapped in a farmhouse in Wantabadgery by police from Wagga Wagga and Gundagai who laid siege to it. In the end James Nesbitt and fifteen-year-old Wernicke were killed, Constable Webb-Bowen was mortally wounded, and the rest of the bushrangers captured alive. No doubt the violent conclusion to Moonlite's brief bushranging career was a sobering indication of the severity with which the Kellys should have expected to be dealt with if such a siege situation were to emerge.

It was at this time that Aaron sold his selection at Sheepstation Creek to Hiram Crawford for £150. No doubt the continuing strained relationship between Aaron and his family had seen him looking to cut ties, and it is likely Aaron would have known that nothing would have dug the boot in deeper to his father than selling the land adjoining the family selection to the enterprising Crawfords.

On 3 December, Nicolson's cave party was officially established and with it came a new phase in the hunt for the gang and Aaron's involvement with it. Though the location of the police camp was never made public, for obvious reasons, it became common knowledge that they were camping in the caves around the Byrne farm. Aaron was now in for a penny and in for a pound, accompanying the police every night as they descended from their cave hideaway to watch the Byrnes for any sign of an arrival of one of the outlaws.

Despite the union causing a fracture in his family, Aaron married Belle Barry in Beechworth on Boxing Day 1879. That morning he visited Paddy Allen, as he often did in his time of need, and asked to borrow some money as he was broke. After lending him some cash, Allen accompanied Aaron to the presbytery where the couple were married by Father Tierney. None of the groom's family were in attendance. In fact, Jack was nearby at a sports meeting at the time the wedding was taking place, blissfully ignorant of the nuptials.

The newlyweds honeymooned over two days, and Detective Ward even gifted them a set of silverware. Afterwards they returned to the Barry household whereupon Aaron immediately resumed his involvement in the police activity. No rest for the wicked, as the saying goes.

13

Boiling Point

Moving into 1880 tensions were high. The police were suspicious of Aaron, the Byrnes had distanced themselves from him and the Lloyds and Quinns were putting pressure on the Kelly Gang to have Aaron taken out. And now on top of that, as Aaron began his married life, his own family had disowned him and were blatantly stirring up trouble.

Jack Sherritt had taken particular umbrage at his elder brother's apparent rejection of his family in favour of the Barrys. He would tell police that they thought too highly of Aaron and complained that he believed that Aaron would receive all of the reward and he would get none. The green-eyed monster soon took over and Jack began to lash out.

In January Aaron took Belle out to ride a merry-go-round; or as some of the time referred to it, a hurdy gurdy. While the couple were out, Jack broke into the Barry house, which had been locked up when the couple left, and stole a gold watch and Belle's new side-saddle, worth £11, that Aaron had purchased on credit from William Willis of Reid Street,

Wangaratta. The stolen items were then planted at the Byrne farm in an outbuilding to throw suspicion onto Paddy Byrne, but Jack was not as clever as he liked to imagine, having seemingly left a tie and collar that was gifted to him by Detective Ward at the scene of the crime. Once Aaron had uncovered the deed, he informed Ward of the crime. Ward seemed unwilling to believe that Jack could have done such a thing and questioned Aaron as to why he thought as he did. According to Ward, Aaron reasoned that it was, "On account of my getting married to Miss Barry."

Ward refused to accept that Jack had stolen the side-saddle and put the tension down to sibling rivalry, perhaps Jack being jealous of his older brother's recent marriage. Anne Sherritt would provide an alibi for Jack, stating that he had also been at the hurdy gurdy, though there seemingly was no corroborative evidence to back this convenient alibi up, and by this time Jack had plenty of practice in establishing questionable alibis for himself.

Nevertheless, Aaron demanded satisfaction and rode to Sheepstation Creek to settle his grievances. Jack, who had been working in one of his father's fields, immediately mounted and took off. Aaron engaged his brother in a horseback chase before he caught up and yanked him off the horse onto the ground. The pair came to blows and, in his rage, Aaron ripped a sapling out of the ground and walloped Jack across the head with it. The blow rendered the younger Sherritt unconscious and bleeding heavily from a wound in the head. Suddenly terrified at the thought that he may have killed Jack, Aaron headed to Paddy Allen's store for a tumbler of whiskey to steady his nerves before turning himself in to the police. Allen plied him with drink and tried to convince him to head over the border instead, but the young Sherritt was determined to do what he considered right.

As this was transpiring, Jack appeared in the doorway behind them covered in blood like a vengeful phantom.

"You bloody wretch, you thought you'd murdered me," the bloodied figure declared.

After a brief moment of tension, a doctor was sent for, Jack's head was stitched up and the brothers were visited in the store by Detective Ward. Ward gave the pair a stern talking to, and the brothers then buried the hatchet, or rather drowned their differences in booze. This amity would not last, nor would it be the last word on the matter of Belle's stolen saddle. Aaron would make it clear to his mother-in-law that it was his belief that Jack had taken the stolen items as he knew that Jack had a down on him.

Trouble once again struck the newlyweds in March, when Aaron and Belle rode into Beechworth on a pair of mares, a chestnut, and a roan, that Aaron had purchased from his father-in-law Ned Barry, which he had paid £2 10s and £3 10s for respectively, nine months before he had begun his courtship. While Belle rode past the Vine Hotel on the roan mare, Aaron stabled the chestnut mare at Paddy Allen's and went about his business in town. When he returned some hours later the horse was gone. He soon discovered that the horses had been seized by the police as they were stolen. In fact, Ned Barry had stolen them and sold them to Aaron shortly before dashing over the border to Wagga Wagga where the police were unable to catch up with him.

The case went to court on 23 March and though Aaron produced a receipt for the sale of the horses the magistrate considered that he knew fully well that the animals were stolen and issued Aaron a fine of £2 2s. It was yet another nasty blow against the embattled couple as they tried to start their new life together.

On 1 April 1880, the cave party was finally disbanded. Months of camping in the mountains had produced no results and the police force was under intense pressure to be seen to be in active pursuit of the outlaws, despite there being no substantial leads to follow. Moreover, the cave party was hardly as secret as the police liked to believe; not helped by members of the police party seen visiting the Sherritt selection from time to time, and the Sherritts themselves visiting the Byrnes. Detective Ward directed the constables on how to report to Nicolson in such a way as to hide from him the fact that it was publicly known that police were camped in the caves near the Byrne selection, but the ineptitude of the operation continued.

On 2 April Constable Falkiner wrote to Mullane stating that he wished to report to Nicolson that "the Sherritts have been continually backwards and forwards together at Byrne's, and as much as sleeping together, and, from their intimacy together, it has been impossible to say this duty has been unknown to the outlaws' friends."

The end of the cave party was a major shift for Aaron, whose lifestyle for the past year had been focused on chaperoning the police. He now found himself with a young wife, living with his in-laws, and suffering a strained relationship with his family and friends, and no secure occupation.

Just after the police abandoned their camp in the cave, Anne, and John Sherritt, under the direction of Ward, took a dray up to the hideaway at night to clear away anything that could give away the location of the camp and in turn throw suspicion on the Sherritts. What they found was a deplorable mess of empty bottles and tins, discarded blankets, and oilskin coats. They cleared away as much as they could, but one item managed to slip away before they had a chance to intercept it. A letter from Constable Falkiner had blown downhill waiting to be found by the Byrnes and their sympathisers. Over the course of the following weeks some of the tins and miscellaneous items the police had littered about the place that had been missed by John and Anne were discovered by the Byrnes, who were able to deduce where the police had camped. Though the Sherritt family appeared to avoid being suspected of involvement, there is no doubt that the placement of the police camp made it obvious to Margret that someone close to the family must have shown the police where to go and that list was very short.

Nicolson's time leading the hunt was also drawing to a close. The animosity between him and Standish was bubbling over, and the Chief Commissioner had been looking for an excuse to take him out of Kelly Country and put Hare back in charge. Hare had been knocking back Standish's requests, citing that there were more senior superintendents in the colony than himself that would be better suited. No doubt Hare was still licking his wounds but also humbly, and wisely, acknowledging his shortcomings in the field. Standish refused to budge and allocated Hare to take over from Nicolson at the beginning of June.

A very telling anecdote from this time shows the state of high anxiety that Aaron was living in. When discussing the last days of Nicolson's involvement in the hunt to the 1881 Royal Commission, Sub-Inspector O'Connor would state:

"At last, about a week before Mr. Nicolson was removed, an informer actually saw Joe Byrne and spoke to him. We got word after twelve hours after she saw him, but we had some four, or six hours' heavy rain between. We, Mr. Nicolson, Mr. Sadleir, and my-self, proceeded to Beechworth, and there saw Aaron Sherritt, who begged and prayed of Mr. Nicolson not to go out, as he himself had tried to follow the tracks of Joe Byrne, and found that they went from where Joe was seen to his (Byrne's) mother's house, and from thence on to a main road, occasioned by the rain which had washed them out. He also said, if we did not get the outlaws, they would know who had given the information, and would come and murder him and his connections. Mr. Nicolson was very anxious to go out, as he considered it would probably be his last chance, and after working so hard for such a long time he did not like to give it up; but he asked the opinion of all present, namely, Superintendent Sadleir, myself, Senior-Constable Mullane, and Detective Ward, and we all said we considered it would not be justifiable to risk the lives of the informers under the circumstances. This occurred just in the last week of Mr. Nicolson's being up there."

Nicolson's determination to catch the Kelly Gang appeared to trump his consideration for the lives of those who he was using as cogs in his machinations to the extent that it took a committee consensus to dissuade him from putting Aaron's family in jeopardy for the sake of chasing a lead. It is clear from this incident that Aaron was feeling the hatred being levelled against him but was not only concerned for his own safety but that of his family. The Kelly sympathisers were known to intimidate and threaten those who they disliked and were very vocal in their opinions about the gang and the police.

A sympathiser named Frank Harty, one of the men arrested and remanded as part of the failed scheme at the beginning of 1879, infamously bragged that he would fight up to his knees in blood for Ned Kelly. Edward Monk, one of the men who had helped retrieve the bodies of the slain police from Stringybark Creek, frequently received death threats from sympathisers and only days after the remanded sympathisers were released from custody it was reported that he had been shot at. Whether he would come through in Ned's hour of need remained to be seen, but there is no doubting the psychological effects of such bellicose and violent preaching, clearly intended to put the opposition on edge.

On Nicolson's last day on the hunt, he investigated a reported citing of Joe Byrne at Sebastopol. Accompanied by O'Connor, his native police, and Sadlier, he rendezvoused with Aaron who guided them through the gully to the Byrne homestead. It soon emerged that the report of Joe Byrne walking a bullock through the gully was in fact a case of mistaken identity, as it was Paddy Byrne who had been spotted. As much as Nicolson may have hoped for a small success on his last day, it was not to be. Furthermore, it soon came to light that Aaron's presence with the party had not gone unnoticed. Archibald Batchelor, who had remained a staunch sympathiser of Joe Byrne and his family, had taken note of the large group of mounted police and trackers and spied them making their way to the Byrne selection through a gully. No doubt this information made its way back to the gang very quickly.

If Aaron harboured ill-feeling towards Nicolson thereafter, it was unclear to those who spoke to him in the period directly after the irascible superintendent's departure from the district. As usual, it seemed as if there was a different version of Aaron for every man that knew him.

Constable Armstrong would state that Aaron told him that, "Nicolson is as cute as a fox; he would know your thinking. He would walk into the mouth of a cannon. I parted with him in Benalla, good friends, and he shook hands with me. This is his cap he gave us; I am wearing it; he gave his cap to me on leaving Benalla."

It is unclear when Aaron finally made the move to the hut at the Devil's Elbow to establish a home for himself and Belle, but it seems they had settled in around the end of February. It was nothing grand, merely an abandoned miner's hut located conveniently between the Woolshed

Falls and Sebastopol. The scrubby piece of land was bordered on one side by the road into El Dorado, and behind the property was a mountain known as the Sugarloaf. The hut itself was fairly non-descript. In fact, so non-descript was it that the police who spent time there could not seem to agree on simple things like what the walls were made of. Based on the descriptions, it seems that the interior walls were wattle-and-daub, with wood cladding on the outside, probably weatherboards. The hut was divided by a wooden partition into two rooms with a wooden floor. There were two doors on opposite sides of the building that opened in such a way as to create a cross-breeze. A singular fireplace was built into the centre of the back wall. The windows were very small and allowed very little light inside. The roof was made from wooden shingles. Between the front of the hut and the road was a large hole that superficially resembled a wombat burrow but was actually the mouth of a tunnel that led down to a creek. This tunnel had seemingly been dug by the original owner of the land to allow direct travel to the creek where they would engage in alluvial gold mining. Evidently the gold deposits in the area were not sufficient and the hut had been sitting abandoned for a considerable time.

As Aaron tried to make the new house a home, he received assistance in clearing and fencing the property from his brother Willie. Though things were still tense between Aaron and his family, Willie had stuck by him and the Sherritt sisters would visit to bring Willie supplies. There was a certain irony in Aaron taking possession of the abandoned hut. It was not that long ago that he had been helping Ned Kelly and Joe Byrne in their crusade against the squatters, and now Aaron found himself imbued with that title himself, albeit with far less grandeur.

The Kelly Gang continued to visit the Byrne selection to gather supplies and in one instance around the time that the cave party had disbanded they were spotted by one of the Sherritt girls who happened to be riding by at just the right time. As Anne Sherritt would later relate:

"...This night she called [at Mrs. Byrne's] on her way home, and who should come up but Joe Byrne, leading a horse, and Dan Kelly. Each of them was leading one and riding another. Mrs. Byrne then came out — there was a whistle — it is a very thick scrubby place, and after a little bit Ned Kelly and Hart came on foot, from the back of the place like, and those two came up the front of the house like, so, and got their provisions. There was some bread and I think it was boiled bacon, and then Patsy Byrne went up the Woolshed and he brought down something in a bottle and gave it to them, and Patsy — Joe Byrne's brother — said, "Which way did you come?" and Joe says, "The way we always come. We came down the steepest part of Wall's Gully.""

The nature of that "something in a bottle" can only be speculated upon, however it is probable that this would have been a supply of laudanum. Laudanum was a tincture of morphine and opium that was widely used as a powerful painkiller. It was extremely effective in this regard and proved useful for women during their monthly cycle in the days before drugs such as paracetamol and ibuprofen. However, being such a powerful opiate made it extremely addictive and lethal overdoses were a sad reality of the time. With Joe being on the run and low on funds it would not be unreasonable to assume that he was unable to procure the opium he habitually smoked, so a substitute needed to be found. Opiate withdrawals can be as fatal as they are unpleasant, with sweating, diarrhoea, stomach cramps, and mood swings among the various symptoms. Laudanum was easily procured, and although taking it was not exactly the same experience as smoking opium tar, the drug would have been effective in curbing Joe's withdrawals in the event that he was unable to get his fix.

Joe's connections to the Chinese at Sebastopol continued to prove useful, though he soon discovered that some of the Chinese had begun to view him with the same suspicion that they had cast upon Ah Suey, Ah Fook and Ah On in those early days. Joe's visits to Yee Fang's store to buy opium tar and other supplies became less frequent as his infamy rose and his funds depleted. Jack Sherritt would later claim that Yee Fang would speak ill of Joe to him following a visit to the store:

"He can talk very good English; I can understand every word he says. He called Joe Byrne Ah Joe, and my brother was known as Ah Jim; they could not say Aaron. He said, "Last night me see Ah Joe come along with Ah Jim to the store." He said, "Him welly bad man before he shot policeman; him shoot policeman and kill him Chinaman." They got a bottle of gin and some tobacco, and something else, and went away. You might think that my brother was with them, but the police knew where he was with them this night; but this man it appeared to me was Ned Kelly who was with them; Joe Byrne was, no doubt, because the Chinamen knew him well, because he used to pelt them and hammer them with stones."

There is no evidence to suggest that Joe had killed any Chinese people before or after what happened at Stringybark Creek, and there is a distinct possibility that the dialogue is completely made up. Certainly, Jack's claim that Joe used to hammer the Chinese with stones is a rather inaccurate reference to the Ah On incident, so the reliability of the account is severely in doubt.

It was known that Joe Byrne had many sympathisers scattered around the Woolshed and surrounding areas that provided him with food and other supplies. One of these was his old sweetheart Ellen Byron, who it seems still carried a torch for the outlaw despite having gotten married. Ellen's husband was a habitual drunk who was frequently before the courts, and it is no far stretch to suggest that the marriage was hardly a fairy-tale arrangement. Ellen would provide Joe with bundles of supplies and act as an intermediary, forwarding notes around between sympathisers and the gang. This was just one of Joe's steadfast supporters, however.

Though the supporters of the gang were known as Kelly Sympathisers, and were referred to as such at the time, support for the gang around the Woolshed seemingly had far less to do with Ned Kelly than with Joe Byrne. It is quite unlikely that people like the Batchelors would have thrown their support behind the outlaws if it were not for Joe being amongst them. The Kellys were not especially known or liked so far north of their stomping grounds around Greta and Wangaratta, as their presence in Beechworth was usually due to attending court as witnesses or defendants. Thus, it seems unlikely that there would have been any notable support base for them without a local boy getting mixed up with them.

On 13 May, Aaron found himself in the Wangaratta Police Court as defendant against William Willis, still having not paid him for Belle's stolen side-saddle. John Phelan appeared as a witness for the prosecution and reported seeing Aaron at the Beechworth Savings Bank with a roll of bank notes amounting to £16 or £18 pounds. He claimed that Aaron said he would never pay Willis and that later Aaron was heard around the Woolshed claiming he would make it hot for Phelan as he had "got [Joe Byrne] inside." In the end the court found in favour of the plaintiff and Aaron was ordered to repay Willis in full, plus the £2 2s 6d court costs or face a month in gaol. Unfortunately for Willis, due to imminent events, the money would not be forthcoming.

14

A Final Changing of the Guard

In early June, James Wallace found himself extracted from his plum position at Hurdle Creek. Suspicions had been raised to Thomas Bolam, the Inspector-General of the Education Department, as to Wallace's supposed sympathies to the outlaws owing to his history with Joe Byrne. Hurdle Creek and Bobinawarrah are situated in close proximity to Greta, Wangaratta, Sebastopol and Beechworth, and a man working part time between two schools and as a postmaster would have plenty of opportunity to travel and provide information to a band of outlaws that he was sympathetic to in those areas.

Wallace had also been sending letters to the Education Department since the end of 1879 demanding that he be placed at the new state school at Benalla East, which was due to open in 1880. Bolam corresponded with Captain Standish and Chief Secretary Robert Ramsay before deciding to relocate Wallace to the school at Yea full-time, away from the direct proximity of the gang's haunts. Upon receiving the news of his imminent transfer, Wallace demanded that one of his brothers should be hired to fill his position at Hurdle Creek, but this was refused by the department. If Wallace had indeed been assisting the gang, he was no longer in a position to do so, and he was also now significantly hampered in his efforts to gather information from the sympathisers to sell to the police.

On 2 June, Superintendent Hare arrived in Benalla to resume control of the hunt for the Kelly Gang. It was a job he took on with diminished zeal, which only continued to diminish once he realised the problems he had inherited. Hare spent a considerable amount of time playing catch-up, going through Nicolson's notes. In particular, Hare found the reports of the outlaws stealing parts of farming tools to make "jackets" to be ludicrous and attributed part of Nicolson's lack of success to the reliance on such bizarre reports.

On top of this, Nicolson had sent a telegraph to Senior-Constable Mullane in Beechworth on the evening that Hare took over from him as the head of the pursuit, informing him to dismiss all of the "secret-service" men in the area, including Aaron Sherritt. Hare immediately ordered Detective Ward to countermand the dismissals.

Hare decided that watch parties must remain a key component of his methodology, and to this end he formed a four-man party to be based in Wangaratta to spy on the Hart family selection, and another based at the Glenrowan police station to spy on the Kellys in Greta. Given that a considerable portion of the sightings of gang members still seemed to be coming from around the Woolshed, this obviously left a gap. But there was a solution, and it required the complete compliance of Aaron Sherritt.

Aaron was struggling to cope with his new lifestyle, post-cave party. He had, in those few months, thrown himself wholeheartedly into working with the police, if only to maintain the façade that he wanted to catch the outlaws. Though he still passed information on to Detective Ward, there was now the inescapable reality that he was a newlywed man with no support from his own family, no friends he could trust, and no regular income. The news that Superintendent Hare and Detective Ward had a plan that required his assistance must have been welcome.

Hare and Ward arranged to have police constables stationed with Sherritt around the clock. During the day the police party were to stay in the hut to avoid detection, and at night they would accompany Aaron to his watch at the Byrne selection, plugging the gap in surveillance. Ward even procured a calico curtain to hang over the doorway into the bedroom and some blinds to cover the windows so that nobody could see inside the hut. There were to be no more months of camping in freezing cold caves waiting for the outlaws to appear.

The four men assigned to the night watch were Constable Henry Armstrong, Constable Robert Alexander, Constable William Duross and Constable Thomas Patrick Dowling. Come night fall they would split up and meet at the Byrne property for a stake-out until dawn.

Aaron must have seen the value in the plan for himself and Belle as well. Having police with him at all times meant that he would be safe from any sympathisers that tried to harm or kill him while on watch, and that Belle would also be protected when the police were in the hut. When Aaron accompanied the police to the Byrne selection at night, Ellen Barry would come to the hut to keep Belle company until he returned.

Though Hare expressed absolute confidence in the plan, Superintendent Sadleir had misgivings, which he would later recount in his memoirs:

"I had nothing but admiration for Hare's zeal, yet there were matters on which we had opposite views. For instance, he placed four police in Aaron Sherritt's hut, not far from the home of Joe Byrne, one of the gang, in the expectation that they could remain there week after week, without being discovered. I was quite sure that any such expectation was futile, and I endeavoured, but in vain, to dissuade him from the undertaking. Men could not I knew be kept concealed in a two-roomed hut which was already occupied by Sherritt and his wife, especially as the place stood open to a main road."

It wasn't long before security concerns popped up. Belle's younger brother attended school with Joe Byrne's youngest brother Denny, and the two were mates. After school they would often hang out together and on at least one occasion it was believed that they visited Belle in Aaron's hut. Immediately afterwards Constable Armstrong ordered Aaron and Belle not to let her brother back again, especially with Denny Byrne, as there was no telling who would hear of the police presence in the hut as news travelled fast on the bush telegraph.

Armstrong would later express to the Royal Commission that he had a great many doubts about Aaron's truthfulness in regard to whether or not he was in fact in communication with the outlaws. He would recount conversations where Aaron would indicate to him that he had not spoken to any of the gang since he had refused to accompany them to Jerilderie, and even went on to state that he knew the gang were actually hiding in the ranges between Rose River and Gippsland with a fifth member whose identity was unknown to the police. When Armstrong quizzed Aaron about why he would tell Hare a different story to what he would tell everyone else he was said to have replied, "I am as true as

you are; I am just working for the pay I am getting for my wife; I am as
true as you are. I would take some other calling if I were dismissed from
the service of the police. I am getting 7s. a day."

So, who exactly was Aaron telling the truth to? Was he lying to
Armstrong for his own amusement, or was he telling Hare lies to justify
a paycheque? We know that Joe Byrne had sent letters to Aaron in the
time since Jerilderie, and there certainly seems to be evidence to support
the idea that on at least a couple of occasions Aaron did actually meet
with members of the gang. Perhaps by suggesting that the gang were
really out of the district, Aaron thought that it would result in less of
a demand for, or expectation of, results. After all, there was immense
pressure on the police at that time to be seen to be doing something and
producing new information or arrests regularly, if they hadn't captured
the outlaws.

In mid-June, Hare finally reunited with Aaron Sherritt face-to-face,
accompanied by Ward, and began their interaction by stating that he
was sorry to hear that he did not have more success with Nicolson.
Aaron replied that he could not work "for that cranky Scotchman" and
explained that Nicolson was belligerent and distrustful of him, and that
Hare's return was a welcome one. There was a brief discussion of Aaron's
marriage and his parents' disapproval thereof, and Hare enquired about
whether Aaron had any qualms about the watch party stationed in his
home. Aaron seemed unconcerned, stating, "No, I do not. I do not know
any better place where they could be; nobody comes to my house, except
my wife's mother, and they are not likely to inform the outlaws of anything that I am doing."

Of course, things did not go to plan, with constables seen outside
during the day performing chores and relaxing. In addition to this,

Denny Byrne would take note of any tracks he found leading from the Byrne selection. The police in the watch party were not as careful as they ought to have been and when Denny found straps that had been dropped by police, word quickly made its way to the gang.

Members of the watch party would later learn that some of the gang had been visiting the Byrne homestead without detection. Estimates would range from once a week to every ten days, but it was a revelation that raised significant questions about the efficacy of the watch party. After all this time, was Aaron still keeping the police looking in the wrong place to allow Joe and the gang to move freely without scrutiny?

On 18 June, as Aaron was walking with the police to the Byrne selection, they were suddenly chased by a group of Chinese miners when they approached the creek. Constable Armstrong asked what the commotion was about, to which Aaron explained that the Chinese men were afraid they were going to rob the gold stored in their sluice boxes. Armstrong and the other police aimed their guns at the miners, and they scattered. The following morning Armstrong sent Aaron to ask the Chinese about what they saw the previous night, hoping that their cover hadn't been blown. When Aaron returned, he told Armstrong, "It is all right, Harry, the Chinamen say they saw the Kellys last night. I told them not to tell, and they said, 'No [bloody] fear, we know Joe Byrne'." Evidently, the miners had mistaken the gun-toting police for the outlaws, so by a stroke of good fortune there was no need to stress about news that police had been spotted approaching the Byrne selection getting about. Subsequently, the party agreed not to head out again until after dark to avoid a repeat.

Later that same day, Hare expressed to Ward a feeling of uncertainty about the men stationed in Aaron's hut. The pair set out on horseback that evening and rode to the Devil's Elbow where there was no sign of anyone from the road. While Hare waited, Ward went to the hut to see if anyone was in there. He discovered that Duross, Dowling and Alexander were present, but Armstrong and Aaron were missing. When Hare demanded to know where they were. He was told by Constable Dowling that Aaron had stated that it was too light when they initially set off, and all of the troopers except Armstrong had been ordered back to make things less conspicuous. Hare ordered Alexander and Duross to take him to where Aaron and Armstrong were supposed to be.

As they walked, there were moments where they appeared to become lost, but eventually they arrived at the Byrne selection. Hare spotted Aaron lying down under a tree forty yards from the door of the Byrne homestead and roused him. In fact, Aaron had been watching the farm alone, having told all four of the assigned constables to wait until it was darker.
Constable Armstrong appeared a moment later with his rifle shouldered and told Hare that the others had lied about him coming to the Byrne selection as he was actually out gathering firewood. In fact, Dowling had been assisting him in the task prior to the arrival of Hare and Ward. Upon learning that Hare was on his way to the Byrne selection, Armstrong had been ordered by Ward to catch up and inform him of what had actually happened. Hare quizzed Armstrong about his opinion of Aaron's reliability and Armstrong was complimentary. Hare was seemingly unimpressed at his first meeting with Armstrong and drew Aaron away to quiz him privately about Armstrong's suitability. Aaron was complimentary, though expressed some disdain for the other men in the party.

That night Hare joined the men as they watched the Byrne house, talking with Aaron about the hunt and all other topics that came to mind. Aaron again expressed utter confidence in Hare's ability to capture the Kelly Gang.

In the early hours, as the water was freezing in the creeks, Aaron escorted Hare back to the hut. When Hare suggested he join him inside for a spot of tea, Aaron refused, stating he had to get back to the men. Hare found it hard to believe that Aaron could be so dedicated to the job and sat on the bank of the creek for a quarter of an hour to test Aaron, waiting to see if he really was walking back to join the rest of the watch party. When Aaron did not return, Hare was satisfied that he was not putting on some elaborate ruse but was genuine in his desire to assist the police.

Later at the hut, Aaron and Armstrong discussed what had transpired, Armstrong fearing that Dowling giving incorrect information about where they had been made them look bad to their superiors. Aaron suspected his brother may have been putting ideas in Ward's head and replied with frustration, "This is some of Mr. Bloody Jack's work, he is always carrying stories to Ward and Mullane, to say I am drunk at the Chinese camp, and so on; if they come always in this way. I will throw up the job."

On 20 June, Paddy Byrne was spotted spying on Aaron's hut at the Devil's Elbow, peeking through any available crack to see who was inside. The police seemed unsure about how long he had been there or what he had seen but were fairly certain that their cover had not been blown. That day Jack Sherritt wrote to Hare to criticise the methods employed in trying to catch the gang:

> *Dear Sir, — I would like very much to have seen you yesterday, as the outlaw Byrne does be frequently and sleeps in ——'s haystack on Sebastopol. I cannot see how it is that he is not caught before now. His brother Patrick does be out all night and sleeps all day. Mrs. Byrne has their winter flannel and socks all ready to go to them, and she has*

provisions for six families stored by in her house. Sir, I don't want to dictate to a gentleman of your ability, but the plan I would suggest is this — for Patrick Byrne to be watched minutely day and night, as this is a particular time. As long as Aaron has the men down there, they will never do any good, as to my knowledge he lets too many of his mother-in-law's children to his house, and his mother-in-law herself will go there night after night, and will stop sometimes until two o'clock in the morning, and this will be the means of discovering the police, as the Barry children and the Byrne children go to the same school and are on friendly terms. Dear sir, the reason I send you these few lines is this — anything I say up here, they will not listen to it; therefore, I would like to explain matters to yourself. I am certain before long they are going to make another raid; I have not heard yet what it is. I am very busy now, but if you don't succeed, sir, I have a grand plan made up that I think will carry through. I remain yours most respectfully, JOHN SHERRITT, junr.

The following night, the watch party took up their normal positions and settled in. At 11:15pm their attention was grabbed by Paddy Byrne leaving the selection, riding his grey mare at a trot towards Madden's Gap. The night was clear and the moon shining brightly enough that the police could see clearly that it was Paddy. It was the brightness of the moonlight, in addition to the almost incessant barking of the Byrnes' dogs, that convinced the party not to pursue, as they would be easily spotted. They remained in place and anticipated Paddy's return, but by 3:30am when the party headed back to the hut he still had not come back. Armstrong directed Aaron to find out where Paddy had gotten to and pick up any information possible while he ventured into Beechworth to report what had happened. The rest of the police were not entrusted with any of the investigative or reporting duties.

Upon receiving Armstrong's report, Detective Ward rode to Aaron's hut for more information. When he arrived, Aaron was missing and did not return until 5:30pm, having been out gathering intelligence. He had been out since noon retracing the route Paddy took the night before but could find no tracks or signs that Paddy had returned. Ward surmised that Paddy had returned home between 3:30am and noon, having ridden to spy on the Sherritt selection while the watch party were out trying to spy on the Byrnes. He could not determine what motivation Paddy would have had in doing so but, Ward being Ward, he would have had theories.

It was roughly at this time that Paddy was spotted by Belle at the back of the hut towards the Sugarloaf. It seems extremely unlikely that Paddy would be visiting Aaron's hut so frequently without suspecting something was up, yet the police still seemed to be under the impression that everyone was ignorant of the police presence there.

Concurrently, Mrs. Byrne had begun leaving hints that the outlaws were up to something big, having been overheard telling people that they were about to do something that would make the ears of the entire colony tingle. Rumour mills were beginning to go into overdrive in all directions.

With Aaron now considered a traitor by the sympathisers, word reached Joe Byrne that a drunken Aaron Sherritt had bragged that he would shoot Joe dead and defile the body before it was cold. Whether there was any substance to the rumour is uncertain but given Aaron's tendency to boast about his ability to dominate Joe, and the breakdown in their relationship of late, it is not out of the question for Aaron to have made such a vile, vulgar comment, whether it reflected his true feelings or not. No doubt this would have weighed heavily on Joe's mind.

On 24 June, Aaron was taken on a pub crawl by one of the police assigned to his hut. Though history doesn't record which trooper, it seems
likely to have been either Armstrong given the way his relationship with
Aaron had developed. After downing drinks at the Hibernian, they went
to the Vine Hotel. Upon entering around 9:00pm, Aaron spotted Joe
Byrne's girlfriend, a general maid known as Maggie, talking to a miner
in a seemingly flirtatious manner. It was unclear whether his response
to Maggie's apparent flirting with another man was a wounding on his
own part or on the part of Joe Byrne, but it was noticeable enough
to prompt questions from his companion. When asked about what was
wrong, Aaron pointed to Maggie and replied, "That girl sees Joe Byrne
every Saturday night."

After Aaron left the pub, the trooper immediately returned to the bar
and questioned Maggie unsuccessfully. The outlaw's lover had no doubts
as to why she was being interrogated and told the trooper, "The devil
a man could have told you that but Sherritt." Despite the protestations
otherwise, Maggie was steadfast in her assessment and informed the
policeman that "somebody else will soon know, too."

This was no idle threat, and word seemingly found its way back to
Joe Byrne regarding Aaron blowing the lid off his clandestine romance,
likely when he visited Maggie for a romantic evening prior to the gang's
next big outing, which they had been planning in secret. Undoubtedly it
was this final straw that made Joe's mind up about Aaron.

On 25 June William Willis decided to confront Aaron personally
about the non-payment of the debt for the side-saddle. It was now at
the point where Aaron had no choice but to cough up or go to gaol for
a month. Despite the court ruling in May, he had still been waiting to
receive the money but when it was not forthcoming a warrant was issued
against Aaron. The warrant had been handed down through Willis' solic-
itor to none other than John Phelan. Phelan had subsequently sat on it

for three weeks and directed his son to keep track of Aaron's movements, looking for an opportune time to serve the order.

Word reached Willis that Phelan was too afraid of Aaron to serve the order and that as Aaron was guarded by police, he was better off going to serve it himself.

Willis rode to Beechworth and while in town stopped for drinks with a friend who confirmed that it was well known in Beechworth that Aaron had police staying in his house to protect him. He also visited Senior-Constable Mullane and expressed his desire to serve the order on Sherritt. During the conversation Willis divulged that he had heard that Sherritt was protected by a party of police, much to Mullane's surprise. Though Willis would not give the source of his information, Mullane assumed it must have been a member of the cave party from Wangaratta. Mullane offered to take the order to Sherritt, but Willis insisted on taking it to Aaron himself the following day, he just needed to wait for John Phelan to return home as he had since learned he was out of town and Willis could not serve the warrant without getting it from Phelan first.

Incidentally, one of the Sherritt girls had lodged with Willis for eighteen months around the time that the cave party was regularly watching the Byrne property, though it is unlikely that this was where Willis got his information from. Willis would never give away the source of his information for fear that the source may be harmed by Kelly sympathisers, merely stating that it was a man who was a mutual friend of himself and the Sherritts. Regardless, it was abundantly clear that the cat was well and truly out of the bag by now and what would come next was more or less inevitable.

15

The Murder of Aaron Sherritt

By the beginning of June, the Kelly Gang were almost ready to come back into the open with a grand plan that would completely alter the course of their career. It was their intention to lure a special train full of police and trackers from the headquarters at Benalla to be derailed. It was hoped that the pursuit would be called off, and any survivors of the crash could be taken hostage and bartered for the release of Ellen Kelly from prison.

The spot chosen for the sabotage was at a small town called Glenrowan that was *en route* to Beechworth from Benalla. A curve in the line was to be pulled up so that the locomotive would be unable to slow or stop in time to avoid flying off the tracks and down an embankment.

An additional part of the plan that the police had been alerted to but dismissed as they had with so many other leads, was the construction of bulletproof armour. Each of the outlaws had a suit of armour that covered the head, torso, and groin, constructed from plough mouldboards and sheet iron. Ned Kelly would later state that he had intended the armour to protect them while robbing banks, but in this case, it seemed to be insurance in the event that there were survivors from the train wreck.

Unlike in their previous missions, Aaron was not made privy to the plan and for a very good reason — he was a key component of it. There has been considerable conjecture about the gang's true intentions regarding Aaron, but the intended plot most likely boils down to one of two options:

The first, and most popularly accepted, is that Aaron Sherritt would be murdered to provide a lure for the train from Benalla. Presumably the four constables stationed in his hut would remain alive to raise the alarm that would kick off an immediate police response from Benalla, with troopers heading to Beechworth to investigate as soon as possible.

The second potential plot is that it was the police who were the targets, with the alarm to either be raised by Aaron or Belle, or a single trooper left alive by the gang to tell the tale. Potentially this option could have allowed the gang to give Aaron a final ultimatum to pledge his allegiance to them or die a traitor's death if they believed his apparent betrayal was of his own volition.

Among the many comments made by Ned Kelly regarding the Glenrowan plot, those made to Constable Armstrong following his capture certainly give weight to the latter plot being the more likely one. It appears that Ned was convinced that Aaron must have been tortured by the police into betraying him. Armstrong would tell the Royal Commission:

"I can state the admission Ned made to me, Ned Kelly. I escorted him to Melbourne with Inspector Baber and two constables. He said, "Was Senior-Constable Johnson in the hut when

Sherritt was shot?" I said, "No; why do you ask me that, Ned?" He asked me if I tortured Sherritt. He said, "What men were there?" I said, "I am sorry to say I was." He said, "To have gone out in you light [sic] would have been foolhardihood; you would have all been shot but one. It was not our game to shoot you all. We wanted one man to go in and draw the police away from the barracks." There is no doubt whatever but that the outlaws knew we were there."

On 26 June 1880, the day began as any other winter's day. At around 4:00am the watch party returned to Aaron's hut from the Byrne selection and the police bedded down.

During the day Aaron rode to Chiltern to look for some of Ellen Barry's cattle that he believed had been impounded. He was gone for around three hours then rode back.

There was no indication that anything remarkable was going to happen, but much like being in the eye of the storm it would not be long until things would break out into chaos.

That night, the gang split up with Ned Kelly and Steve Hart heading to Glenrowan to tear up the train tracks, while Joe Byrne and Dan Kelly headed to the Devil's Elbow.

Joe and Dan rode with a pack horse in tow, likely carrying weapons and camping gear, and possibly their iron armour.

On the way to Aaron's hut, the pair passed Anton Wick as he was returning home, doubled back and bailed him up. By Wick's account, Joe did not recognise him and asked him to identify himself. Joe then stooped and asked if Wick recognised him. Despite his history with Joe, Wick could not recognise him. When Joe revealed his identity, Wick was in disbelief but when Joe presented a revolver and aimed it at him, he suddenly realised it was true. Wick had a reputation as a brawler, but on this occasion, he was in no position to fight back as Dan Kelly handcuffed him and he was made to accompany the outlaws up the road to Aaron's home.

Joe explained, "Don't be frightened. I won't hurt you. You summoned me once for a horse, but I forgive you that. [...] You have to go with us to Sherritt's place, and you must do what we want, and we will do you no harm."

It is curious that the outlaws initially rode past Wick then doubled back. If bailing Wick up to use him as a lure was part of the plan, as has been asserted by most authors and historians since 1880, it is odd that they would not have stopped him straight away. It also seems very coincidental that they should just happen to find him on the right stretch of road at just the right time, but it could be argued that they had checked for him at his property first, though there was no evidence to suggest that to be the case. Perhaps, unlike what we have assumed to be the case for over 140 years, bailing up Anton Wick was a spur of the moment decision by Joe.

Meanwhile, the police party of Armstrong, Alexander, Dowling and Duross were preparing to head over to the Byrne selection as per the nightly ritual. Armstrong dozed on the bed while Duross warmed his hands by the fire. The others sat in the bedroom preparing their weapons. Aaron sat at the dining table with its apple crate seats, while Belle went about her chores and her mother was also present to keep an eye on Belle in her husband's absence. Apart from the fireplace, the only light in the tiny hut came from a solitary candle burning on the table.

When the outlaws and Wick arrived at Aaron's hut at around 6:00pm, the outlaws hitched their horses and Dan waited at the front door. Joe said to Wick, "You have nothing to do but what I tell you. [...] Me and

you go to the door and knock at it."
Joe went around to the back door with Wick and the prisoner knocked
while Joe hid behind the chimney.

The sudden knocking startled the occupants of the hut but when
Belle enquired who it was, their fears were allayed by the meek reply
with the heavy German accent, "It's Anton Wick. I've lost my way."

Aaron stated confidently that he knew who it was. Constable Duross
retreated into the bedroom, pausing to instruct Aaron to answer the
door and show the old man the way home. Aaron opened the door wide
and peered into the gloom. He pointed, directing Wick to a sapling
in the distance. Suddenly he noticed something, asking quietly, "Who's
that there?"
Without a further word Joe emerged from behind the chimney and shot
Aaron twice with a double-barrelled shotgun. The first shot ripped open
his chest and caused Aaron to lurched backwards. The second shot tore
open Aaron's throat. With gaping wounds gushing with blood, Aaron
staggered, struck his head on one of the apple crate seats as he hit the
floor and died without a word.

Joe stood over the body and stated, "That's the man I want. [...] The
bastard will never put me away again."

It seems that after all those years, through all the high drama with
the outlawry up to that point, Joe still held a grudge against Aaron for
the El Dorado cow incident and the subsequent gaol time. He also stated
that Aaron would no longer be blowing about what he will do to him,
indicating that the rumours of Aaron mouthing off about what he would
do to Joe had indeed reached the gang and helped to sway Joe's decision
to be the trigger man that ended Aaron's life.

Chaos followed as Joe interrogated Belle and her mother as to the identities of the men in the bedroom. Ellen Barry was confident that Joe would not harm them, as she had known Joe for most of his life. In fact, as a child he had slept in the bed between his mother and Ellen. It must have been as surreal as it was terrifying to see that little boy had now grown into the murderer that was standing by the bloodied corpse of her son-in-law.

There was a knock at the front door and Joe ordered Mrs. Barry to open it. The woman did as she was directed and was greeted by Dan Kelly brandishing a pistol. He strode inside and, according to some accounts from the women, he rested his elbow on the table while he looked at Aaron's body and smiled. Joe continued to demand the names of the men in the bedroom, but Ellen would only tell him that there was a man named Duross who was there looking for work. Joe evidently did not believe her and ordered Belle to bring the men out.

Ellen asked Joe why he had shot Aaron, to which Joe replied, "If I did not shoot Aaron, he would shoot me." Ellen followed up by asking to go outside, which was granted, and she spoke with Anton Wick briefly.

The police tried to find a position to get a view out of the room but found no satisfaction. Alexander stood at the doorway with his gun poking through the calico sheet that acted as a partition, and when he attempted to cock it, Byrne could hear it from the other room. He called out, "Hark! Look out; do you hear that? They are cocking their guns."

Joe sent Belle into the bedroom to get the men out. Several times she darted in and out of the room, but the final time, once Belle passed through the curtain into the bedroom, the police kept her there and refused to come out. In frustration, Joe fired through the wall, narrowly missing Belle, who was immediately shoved under the bed and pinned there by the police. Joe then began to yell abuse at the police, stating, "Come out you bloody bastards; I'll shoot you like bloody dogs."

There was now an impasse, for if the police left the bedroom, it would be certain death for them. Whereas the two outlaws, who had decided not to wear their armour, were too vulnerable if they tried to rush into the bedroom.

The outlaws decided to try and flush them out. Joe sent Dan to guard the bedroom window from outside to prevent an escape. While he guarded the window, Dan fired his revolver into the wall, dislodging a chunk of wattle-and-daub inside, which almost struck the cowering police. More shots were fired, but this did not get the police moving as intended.

Joe moved outside and fired a shot at the wall. He sent Ellen in to see if the shot had dislodged anything, which she did. She immediately returned with her report, and they proceeded to engage in a conversation for about ten minutes, during which Joe spoke of his mother among other things that were completely incongruous with the grim situation they were now in, including the time Anton Wick had taken him to court over the stolen horse. When they had finished talking, Joe took Mrs. Barry by the arm and led her back inside.

Meanwhile, Dan had gathered material to start a fire with, but the branches Dan had stacked against the wall were too wet to light and as Ellen walked past with Joe, he asked her for kerosene. She replied there was none, explaining the light inside was from a candle. Joe stated that they intended to burn the place, and Ellen immediately flew into a panic. "Don't, for God's sake, do that, or the girl will be burnt too," Ellen begged.

"You go in and bring her out," Joe replied.

"If I go in, I shan't be let out again, perhaps."

"We will see about that."

Ellen again begged for Joe to relent, stating that she knew he had a soft heart. Joe replied, "I have a heart as hard as stone."
When Mrs. Barry went into the bedroom, the police shoved her violently under the bed next to her daughter and instructed them both to remain quiet.

Outside, Joe and Dan were in deep discussion about what to do. The situation had clearly spun wildly out of control, and they no longer had any clear idea about how to get at the police. Joe raised the idea of sending Anton Wick inside to bring the others out, but Dan shut the idea down.

After two hours, the bushrangers decided to cut their losses. Dan removed the handcuffs from Wick and asked him if his horse was at home. Wick replied that it was not, as it had been turned out. Dan seemed satisfied and ordered Wick not to give any information. The German was happy to oblige and ran home.

The police inside the hut remained convinced the building was hopelessly surrounded by bushrangers, and none of them would emerge from the bedroom until 11:00pm, when Armstrong slinked out of the bedroom to close the front and back doors. He pushed them shut with his gun then rolled firewood across to keep them closed. He immediately returned to the bedroom to wait until dawn.

It is unknown exactly what Joe Byrne and Dan Kelly did after leaving the scene of the crime. There is reason to believe they may have briefly camped before heading to Glenrowan, where they were reported to have arrived at around 5:00am. Subsequent to their leaving, Paddy Byrne roamed the perimeter of the murder hut, keeping watch for anyone coming or going and turning people back from heading into Beechworth.

It can be safely assumed that some of the activity the police took as a sign that the Kelly Gang were outside was most probably due to Paddy's presence.

It is possible that Paddy was unaware of the time-sensitive nature of the gang's plans and by preventing news escaping he unintentionally sabotaged them. It also seems that Paddy had decamped after having given Joe and Dan enough time to put a reasonable distance between themselves and the police if a pursuit was to be made, but none of the parties considered that the police would have been too scared to leave until well after daybreak. This would go on to have even more tragic repercussions very soon.

This portrait of Jack Sherritt was commissioned by Supt. Nicolson along with a matching one of Aaron to identify the brothers in case they were forced into a bank robbery by the outlaws.
[Public Domain]

THE MURDER OF SHERRITT.
(FROM A SKETCH TAKEN IMMEDIATELY AFTER THE DEPARTURE OF THE KELLY GANG.)

The Murder of Sherritt (From a Sketch Taken Immediately after the Departure of the Kelly Gang).

Source: *The Illustrated Australian News, July 3, 1880. [Courtesy: State Library Victoria; IAN03/07/80/97]*

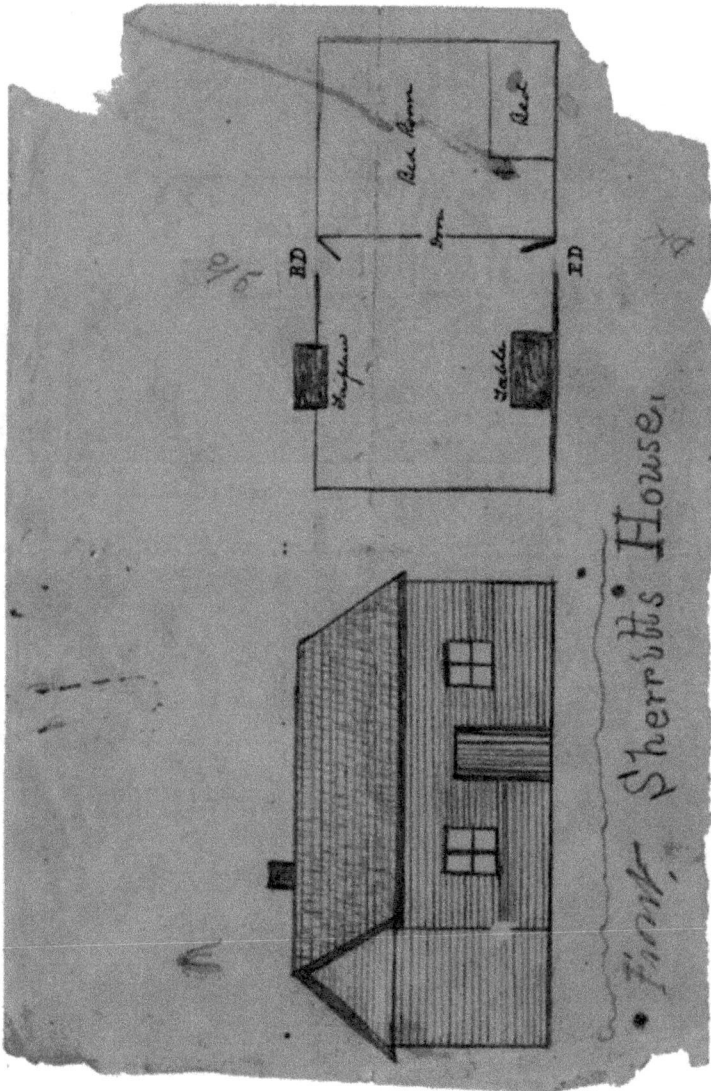

Plan of Aaron Sherritt's house.

[Courtesy: Public Records Office Victoria; Kelly Historical Collection - Part 5:
Miscellaneous Records; VPRS 4969]

The site of Sherritt's Hut at The Devil's Elbow.
[Author's collection]

The granite doorstep from Sherritt's hut.
[Author's collection]

16

Destruction of the Kelly Gang

At the time that Joe and Dan were leaving the Devil's Elbow, Ned Kelly and Steve Hart were in Glenrowan attempting to pull up the rails. Unequipped for the task, they began looking for people that were capable, making prisoners of a gang of gravel collectors, Mrs. Ann Jones and her daughter Jane, the Stanistreet family who lived at the gatehouse, as well as two platelayers. One of the platelayers, James Reardon, later informed the Royal Commission of what had transpired when Ned Kelly had bailed him up:

> "It was twenty minutes past two when I left my house — he took me to break the line; he had a man named Sullivan, a repairer on the line, in charge at the time — that was Ned Kelly, and then I heard the dogs barking, making a row, and I got up and dressed myself and went outside the door, and heard a horse whinneying down by the railway line, and I went towards where I heard the horse. I thought it was the horse of a friend, and I went down, and

Sullivan was coming through the railway fence, and I said, "What is the matter?" and he said, "I am taken prisoner by this man." Ned Kelly came up and put a revolver to my cheek and said, "What is your name?" and I said "Reardon," and he said, "I want, you to come up and break the line" He said, "I was in Beechworth last night, and I had a great contract with the police — I have shot a lot of them, and I expect a train from Benalla with a lot of police and black fellows, and I am going to kill all the —— ——." I said, "For God's sake, do not take me — I have got a large family to look after." He said, "I have got several others up, but they are no use to me," and I said, "They can do it without me," and he said, "You must do it or I will shoot you," and he took my wife and seven or eight children to the station."

This is an intriguing and important piece of information to examine in light of the plan of attack at the Devil's Elbow. Ned specifically said to Reardon, according to this testimony, that a number of police had been shot at Beechworth, which he expected would prompt a response from the police in Benalla. Reardon does not put any particular emphasis on this in the rest of his evidence, but it highlights the probability that Ned was unaware of Aaron's fate because he had sent Joe and Dan to kill the police instead. This tallies up well with what he would later tell Constable Armstrong. If he was expecting Aaron to be murdered, why would he have said it was police that were shot?

By 4:00am at Sherritt's hut, the candle had burnt out, the fire had extinguished, and the police were considering emerging from the bedroom. The occupants of the hut were convinced they could hear voices outside and were afraid the outlaws were waiting outside to ambush them if they walked out. After a little experimentation it was established that the hut was not surrounded and nobody inside was at risk. Armstrong asked the women for a drink, to which request Ellen Barry informed him that there was cold tea on the table from supper. Belle cautioned that Dan Kelly may have poisoned the tea and it was immediately disposed of in the fireplace. Armstrong then sent Mrs. Barry out to fetch water and prepare breakfast for the police.

By the time that Joe and Dan finally arrived in Glenrowan, the tracks had been sabotaged at the bend and all that remained was for the outlaws to lay in wait for the expected police train to come rocketing along the line to its doom. It is unclear if Joe had explained to Ned that Aaron had been killed, or if Ned had even enquired. The gang split their prisoners between the gatehouse and Ann Jones' Glenrowan Inn. While Steve looked after the women and children in the gatehouse, everyone else was kept at the hotel to wait. Joe reportedly took the opportunity to help himself to Ann Jones' best brandy.

At sunrise, around 7:00am, a Chinese man was passing by Aaron's hut and Armstrong summoned him. He gave him a note to give to the police in Beechworth, and the man headed off. Only a few minutes had passed when the man soon returned with the note, stating that he was too busy to go into Beechworth. Armstrong had to think quickly and knowing that the school was a short walk from the hut, he ordered the Chinese man to take the note to Cornelius O'Donoghue, the schoolmaster. As incentive, he gave the man five shillings. Once again, the man returned, claiming now that he was afraid that he would be shot. Though he did not state as much, it is possible that Paddy Byrne had intercepted him along the road and threatened him. He handed back the note but retained the money.

Eventually, Cornelius O'Donoghue was notified and came by the property from the school and said he would raise the alarm. However, half an hour later he returned, stating he could not go as his wife feared she might be murdered before he came back.

In the end, a local miner named Duckett agreed to raise the alarm, but after two hours with no further communication from Duckett, Armstrong decided to head out himself on foot, having failed to locate any of Aaron's horses. It was now around 9:00am.

As this farce was unfolding at El Dorado, the outlaws continued to wait for the police train, but as the day wound on, they found that they had to continue adding prisoners to the existing number in order to prevent interference. Prisoners were allowed to dance and partake in sports, with Ann Jones providing the food.

In the gatehouse, Steve Hart got drunk and napped on the sofa with his pistols resting on his chest. The grand plan was not going well.

As Armstrong walked, he had made it around a mile up the road when he spotted Paddy Byrne on his grey horse. At first, he assumed it was Joe Byrne, but would later learn that Joe was at that time in Glenrowan with the other outlaws. Paddy charged at him then turned off the road.

With no means of transport, and another three miles still to go to Beechworth, Constable Armstrong bailed up a gentleman named Considine on the road and commandeered his horse. It was now midday, and the old nag was quickly getting knocked up from riding.

It was not until around 1:00pm that Constable Armstrong finally arrived in Beechworth to inform Detective Ward of Aaron's murder. He initially spoke to Mullane, but upon learning of the outrage, Ward wasted no time in sending word out. The telegraph, it eventuated, was disrupted between Beechworth and Benalla, so he would have to wait for a reply from Captain Standish in Melbourne, but time was running out.

Soon after news of the murder had been sent by telegraph, Magistrate Foster was summoned to act as coroner on the body. He rode out to El Dorado where around 100 people were milling around the murder hut trying to see inside. Foster entered and found it too dark to see. He would describe the situation to the Royal Commission in 1881:

"I said, "I want a light." [the constable] said, "Well, we do not care much about a light here, sir." I said, "Well, you must get it." A light was then procured. While the light was being got I said, Where is the body?" and one of them said "You are almost stand-ing on it." I turned round, and by this time my eyes had become accustomed to the darkness, and I saw the corpse close to me. I distinguished the man's teeth, and one of his eyes, all the rest was blood. I then interrogated the men there, two or three of them, and I also spoke to Mrs. Barry, made such enquiry as I could. I cannot remember exactly what questions I put, but they were with the object of ascertaining how the thing occurred, and how it came that the police had not made any attack upon the Kellys. [...] My opinion is, had the men made a rush and gone out they would have met a certain death, because [Byrne and Kelly] had only to step a yard or two back and they would be invisible on account of the darkness of the night. The police would naturally suppose there were four outlaws there. This room, according to the enquiry I made immediately after, had had a bright fire in it, and a lighted candle. One of the constables stooped down and pointed to the left eye of the corpse and said, "That is where he got his death wound." As a matter of fact, I learned at the inquest that he received two shots; one entered just above the collar bone and passed backwards through his body, the other went in just above the navel and broke two ribs and went through the kidney. I took that to be the second shot, and he fell back then. As a matter of fact, he had no wound in the head at all, but it looked just as if that was where he had been shot, as it was covered with blood."

Completely by accident, the delay in a police response had thrown Ned Kelly's plan out of the window. Had the train gone through Glenrowan on the Sunday morning as expected, it would most likely have derailed, and the outlaws would have succeeded in carrying out the rest of their plan. Instead, the hold up in reporting Aaron's death meant that the gang had to guard almost the entire town for the duration of the Sunday, split between the gatehouse and the Glenrowan Inn, becoming increasingly sleep deprived and intoxicated from alcohol consumption.

The police train eventually arrived at Glenrowan railway station in the early hours of Monday morning, having been warned about the damaged tracks by the local schoolteacher, who Ned had allowed to take his family home the evening before. Upon learning the outlaws were in Jones' inn, Superintendent Hare led his party to the spot and a gunfight broke out.

Hare retired from the fight early on with a shattered wrist after being shot, leaving the police without a clear chain of command. The outlaws, dressed in their armour, survived the massive volley of gunfire aimed at them, though Ned was badly wounded in his left arm and foot, and Joe was shot through the calf rendering him unable to walk.
The gang retreated, Dan and Steve continuing to fire from inside the inn while Ned and Joe discussed their plan at the rear. Ned then escaped from the far end of the property into the bush, where he fell unconscious. By the time his regained consciousness his path back to the inn had been cut off by the arrival of police reinforcements.

At 5:30am on 28 June 1880, Joe Byrne heaved himself up on the bar of

Ann Jones' inn and poured himself a drink. He gave a toast to the Kelly Gang and was almost immediately killed when a police bullet passed through a gap in his armour. His femoral artery was severed, and he bled to death within two minutes.

Just before dawn, Ned Kelly emerged from the bush and engaged the police in a battle. He was quickly brought down by a shot to his unprotected knee and taken into custody clinging to life.
Some of the civilians had escaped early in the siege while being shot at by police, with the remainder being allowed to emerge at 10:00am. Now the only living people in the besieged inn were Dan Kelly and Steve Hart, with a wounded civilian, Martin Cherry, trapped in the detached kitchen.

After news of Aaron's shooting had spread through El Dorado and reached his family, Jack Sherritt took up arms and joined a detachment of police headed to Glenrowan from Beechworth that included the police from the watch party. By the time Jack arrived on the scene to avenge his brother's death, Ned Kelly was in police custody, Joe Byrne was dead, and Dan Kelly and Steve Hart were not long for the world.

That afternoon, the Glenrowan Inn was burned down by police in a poorly conceived effort to smoke the outlaws out. The bodies of Dan and Steve were partially cremated, but Joe's body was dragged clear by police, one of whom was Constable Armstrong, before the flames could do too much damage to it.

The Kelly Gang had finally been destroyed.

Aaron's inquest was held in the Vine Hotel on the same day as the Glenrowan siege before Magistrate Foster. Among the jurymen were Paddy Allen and James Ingram who had known the deceased so well in life.

John Sherritt was brought in to identify the body, merely stating:

"I am a farmer and dairyman, and live at Sheep-station Creek. I have seen the body outside the court. It is the body of my son Aaron Sherritt. His age was 25 years; I do not know from personal knowledge how he came by his death."

Other witnesses at the inquest were Willie Sherritt, Ellen Barry — who described the events of the previous night — and Dr. Dobbyn who gave his medical assessment on the cause of death:

"I have this day made a post-mortem examination of the body outside the court. It is the body of an adult 5ft. 11½ inches high and about 23 years of age. I found a bullet mark, on the left side of the waistcoat, corresponding to a hole in the neck. There was an opening in the left side of the neck above the collar bone about an inch in diameter. I traced the wound from left to right, it had severed the jugular. I traced it across the windpipe to the right side, where it had smashed one of the ribs to pieces. There was a wound in the right shoulder immediately below the joint. There was another wound in the left breast about two and a half inches below the nipple. The wound corresponded with the opening in the clothes. On opening the body, I traced the wound under the stomach, across the spine, under the right kidney and out immediately above the pelvis. Found the ribs were driven inwards on the left side. Detected no wound in the face, although it was covered with blood. Neither was the skull injured. The ventricles of the heart were completely empty of blood. The gunshot wounds, as described, was the cause of death. The body was healthy. Could find no bullets in the body."

In the absence of the police from the watch party, who were at that moment in Glenrowan helping bring an end to the Kelly outbreak, the inquest was adjourned until the following Wednesday.

That evening Aaron's body was taken to Beechworth cemetery in an inexpensive coffin, procured in haste, and buried in an unmarked plot. The rudimentary funeral was presided over by Reverend J. G. Mackie and only attended by Belle and a "few near relatives", most likely Ellen Barry, John and Willie Sherritt.

The day after Aaron's funeral, Joe's corpse was strung up against a cell block at the Benalla police station for photographs. In a cell nearby Ned Kelly was being held, awaiting transfer to Melbourne Gaol where he would recuperate until he was well enough to return to Beechworth for his committal hearing. Captain Standish would unofficially give photographers permission to photograph Byrne's decaying body to provide an adequate distraction for the police to extract Ned and take him to the train station without a huge crowd. It would be reported that when Ned Kelly eventually returned to Beechworth to face his committal hearing, he doffed his hat to two women on the balcony of the Empire Hotel. Those two women were Belle Sherritt and her mother.

In the close-up portraits of Byrne, he appears strangely serene, as if merely sleeping. There is no indication on his face of his gruesome death. The rest of the body is a different matter. The clothes are untucked, shredded, or bloodstained, the hands are clenched and covered in dried blood, the rings of the slain policemen Lonigan and Scanlan still visible on his fingers. Both Joe and Aaron had died violently, but only Joe would have the indignity of having his remains strung up on a door like a salami for people to gawp at.

After the body was taken down, a post-mortem was done in haste and in secret, and the body buried in a pauper's grave in Benalla cemetery before it could be claimed. The police did not want a repeat of the situation with the charred remains of Dan and Steve, which had been handed to the family who buried them in unmarked graves. The wake for the outlaws had seen around 200 people crowd Maggie Skillion's selection in Greta. Many of the attendees were drunk and armed.

Casts of Joe's head and hands had also been made for Max Kreitmayer's waxworks in Melbourne prior to the burial. The mud and blood en-crusted boots were also taken for the waxworks to be displayed with the wax likeness of the bushranger made from the castings. What became of Joe's other possessions, including the rings of the slain constables, remains a mystery.

When Aaron's inquest resumed on the Wednesday, evidence was gathered from Anton Wick, Belle Sherritt, Constable Armstrong, Constable Alexander, and Ellen Barry was re-examined. Finally, the official verdict was that Aaron Sherritt was murdered by Joe Byrne, abetted by Dan Kelly.

17

Aftermath

On 1 July, John Sherritt wrote to Superintendent Hare, hoping to gain assistance in having his sons recruited into the police force. In the wake of Aaron's murder, tensions were high and not only did the police force potentially provide the boys with protection, but it could also provide them with successful careers:

> *Mr. Hare*
>
> *Dear Sir*
>
> *You have heard of the murder of my Dear Son Aaron it Seems the mother or the Son Patsy is not satisfied yet On Monday last Aaron's burial took place on the night – Tuesday night their was five or six signals given about five or six perches of my house those signals is whistles after a little while, came a foot step close to the door went out and seen the man running a way could not tell who it was but I have come to the Conclusion it must be the murders Brother Coming to see if my son John was about these signals is the same that the murder had when in the*

ranges it was about eight aclock at night when this took place. the reason
of this is on the day of Aaron's funeral it was Commonly ..... reported in
Beechworth that it was my son John that shot Burns at Glenrowan but
my son John is stooping with the Police in Beechworth and is a fraid to
Come home also his Brother William is going up to stop with the Police
until we hear from you On the Saturday night that Joe Burns murdered
Aaron Burns says to Aaron's mother inlaw to send out Johny Sherritt he
want him Mrs. Barry said he was not here Send me out William Sherritt
She Said William was not their my son William was just half an hour
...... left to come home when the murder took place my son – William was
working down on the Woolshed he sleps in Aaron's house at night ecept
on a Saturday night when he would Come home to see his mother

I have reported those signals to Detective Ward and also to the Police
Magistrate on this day the two young lads want to leave the ovens district and made up their mind to join the police John is 21 years William
going in to 20 years and if you would be so very kind as to Speak of it
to the Chief Commissioner to take them on you – / will be the means
to keep them from being murdered the two lads will have to stop at the
Police Camp until the hear from you Detective Ward was say it would be
better for Johny to go to New Zealand and join the Police their but their
mother will not let them go their, when the learn their drill the could be
sent to gelong where my Brother George was Stationed about Seventeen
years ago he was Stationed under Sergent Glass when those boys leaves
me I will have none to help me I have seven Daughters and one Son the
son nineteen months old we give all the information that we could get
about the Kelly Gang to Detective Ward and after all I have lost my
Dear Son that I will never forget and it will be the means of shortening
my wifes days

Dear Sir I hope you are not seirously – wounded, thank god that the
murders is at an end my wife says that you will do what you can to

protect her two boys the are at the Police Camp in Beechworth until the
hear from you
   I remain Yours
   most
   respectfully
John Sherritt

Jack and Willie Sherritt would subsequently be recruited into the police force, partly on the recommendation of Superintendent Hare, who apparently had never actually met them and made the recommendation largely based on how highly Aaron had spoken of them, as well as a sense of obligation to the Sherritt family after the service to the police force that cost Aaron his life. Unfortunately, the brothers were deemed a poor fit for the force and Superintendent Nicolson kicked them out in October 1880. Jack and Willie were given no grounds for their dismissal and immediately sought assistance to get back into the force, but Nicolson had obviously heard along the grapevine what they were up to. In a statement by Jack that was published in the press in December 1880 he stated that:

"Mr. Nicolson telegraphed for us from Melbourne. We went in to see him. He asked us if we had made up our minds to clear out of the colony, and where we were going. I told him that we were waiting for a reply from our parents as to what we had better do. He said, 'There is no occasion to wait for them; you are old enough to judge for yourselves;' and directed us to clear out at once, as we could not stop at the depot, stating that if I remained about Richmond I would get into gaol in three month; and 'Don't attempt to use any political influence in the matter.' I and my brother cannot with any safety go home to Beechworth.

We have no home and no money, except 11s and 6d. My father and my mother have besides us, eight children to support. I and my brother have lost our selections and given up our contract."

Nicolson attempted to have the brothers offloaded to the New South Wales police, but they refused to take what they considered to be rejects from an inferior police force.

Unemployed and unable to return to live with his parents for fear of being attacked or killed by Kelly sympathisers, Willie went to Queensland with letters of recommendation to join the police force but was again refused work. A letter from Willie at the time explains that the reference letter from Nicolson was poorly written and inaccurate, and he indicates that bullying from Nicolson and other police during his brief stint in the Victoria Police had a lasting and adverse effect on him.

Jack begged, unsuccessfully, to be let back into the police force. Subsequently he went to South Australia where he was injured falling from a horse but was able to find word as a ploughman and butcher. He and Willie both lodged complaints about the way that they were treated by Victoria Police, and this was partly responsible for the creation of the 1881 Royal Commission into the conduct of the Victoria Police in relation to the Kelly outbreak. When Jack testified during the Royal Commission, he had no qualms in using it as a platform to try and publicly attack the police and Nicolson particularly, still harbouring considerable resentment about the treatment he and his brother had received at his hands. Jack would continue to express a desire never to return to Kelly Country for fear that he would be murdered by sympathisers. He feared Mrs. Byrne in particular.

Over the next year, Belle abandoned the hut she had lived in with her murdered husband and moved back in with her parents. She sought reparations from the police for their culpability in Aaron's death, being granted a weekly pension of ten shillings. Shortly after the murder she suffered a miscarriage and subsequently endured poor health. She received no support, financial or otherwise, from Aaron's family.

The relationship with her family became strained and she was forced to moved out of home. She rented a room in Beechworth for five shillings a week, leaving her only half of her income to cover all of her other expenditures. This caused public outcry, and in September of 1881 Ellen was granted twenty shillings a week until the end of June the following year, as well as arrears amounting to £82.

In 1884, Ellen married Michael Murphy, proprietor of the Woolpack Hotel in Corowa, to whom she bore four children. In February 1902 Murphy was taken to court for desertion, having abandoned the family twelve months earlier but the case was settled out of court.

On 29 November 1880, Margret Byrne and her sons Paddy and Denny were arrested over Belle's stolen side-saddle, which was found in an outbuilding on the Byrne selection while police were executing a search warrant looking for jewellery. They were charged with larceny and when the case went to court in early December, insufficient evidence was found to pin the theft on the Byrnes and the charges were withdrawn. It was later generally accepted by police that it was Jack that had stolen and planted the saddle, though Constable Armstrong would insinuate to the 1881 Royal Commission that it was a set-up by Detective Ward.

In the years following the outbreak, the Byrnes moved to Albury in an attempt to start fresh. Misfortune would follow them over the border and Kate Byrne was institutionalised after attempting to murder her mother. Kate displayed symptoms of severe mental illness, possibly schizophrenia, and was admitted to the lunatic asylum in Albury where she remained until she died as an old woman, alone and forgotten.

Many years after the outbreak, Jack Sherritt and Paddy Byrne had a public reconciliation in Beechworth to bury the hatchet between the two families that had been so terribly affected by their roles in the Kelly outbreak. Paddy would be found dead sometime later having drowned after a muster. There was no sign of foul play, and the prevailing belief was that it may have been a suicide, if not simply a bizarre accident.

Following the siege of Glenrowan, Ned Kelly was rehabilitated in Melbourne Gaol. He survived long enough to stand trial for the murder of Constable Lonigan, for which he was found guilty and sentenced to death. Despite protests and a petition seeking a reprieve, he was hanged on 11 November 1880. His body was dissected, and the remains buried in the gaol grounds until its demolition in the 1920s. He was never recorded as having admitted to arranging Aaron's murder as part of his grand plan at Glenrowan, in fact he demonstrated confusion about reports that it had been done.

Over time, the myths of the Kelly story resulted in Aaron Sherritt being unfairly vilified as an outright traitor; a self-serving fizzgig. Such a negative association with Aaron's name blackened his character, despite him being a victim of the politics of the Kelly story rather than an antagonist. Sadly, not only did the police's carelessness make Aaron a target, but their terrible decisions helped lead the outlaws to murder him and meant that his death was not reported for more than twelve hours, which could have led to the murderer getting away were it not for the Glenrowan plot. That the police in question were demoted or sacked afterwards was little comfort to Belle and the rest of the Sherritts.

Aaron Sherritt has suffered a tremendous injustice due to the inaccuracies in the telling of the Kelly story through the years. Whereas he was traditionally portrayed as some kind of "Beechworth Judas", his story highlights, more than any other, the true nature of the network of Kelly Sympathisers. While many were sincere in supporting the cause and the gang, the majority were bandwagon riders that hoped for reflected glory and a share of the loot whenever a bank was robbed. The truth is that the sympathisers are directly responsible for Aaron's murder and the chain of events that followed, resulting in no less than six untimely deaths. If misinformation about Aaron being a traitor had not been spread as gospel truth, quite contrary to the reality, the gang would have had a different path roll out for them.

The final resting place of Aaron Sherritt - an unmarked grave in Beechworth Cemetery.
[Author's collection]

Not far from Aaron's grave is that of Anton Wick and his wife.
[Author's collection]

The grave of Joe Byrne in Benalla Cemetery; with the other three outlaws in unmarked graves in Greta, Byrne's final resting place is often treated as a shrine by self-proclaimed "Kelly Sympathisers".

[Author's collection]

A contemporary illustration of the Royal Commission into the conduct of the police force, partially prompted by allegations made by Jack Sherritt. Included in the image are Captain Standish, Superintendent Hare, Acting Commissioner Nicolson and Sub-Inspector Stanhope O'Connor.

Source: The Australasian Sketcher, April 23, 1881. [Courtesy: State Library Victoria; A/S23/04/81/129]

Aaron Sherritt
Source: The Illustrated Australian News, July 3, 1880. [Courtesy: State Library Victoria; 1760484]

Timeline

- August 1855 – *Aaron Sherritt born*

1870-76

- September 1872 – *Aaron Sherritt's butcher's licence is granted, then revoked.*
- 1872 – *Aaron is caught out attempting to used his friend Ah Loy to procure a false butcher's licence for him.*
- 20 September 1873 – *Aaron begins the process of selecting land near his parents' selection at Sheepstation Creek*
- February 1874 – *Aaron's selection application is granted.*
- August 1874 – *Aaron appears as a witness in the trial of James and Daniel Kelty*

1876

- 20 May 1876 – *Aaron and Joe steal a cow from the El Dorado Common School, slaughter and butcher it.*
- 30 May 1876 – *Joe and Aaron stand trial on charges of illegal possession of a carcass. Found guilty, they are sent to Beechworth Gaol for six months.*
- 6 November 1876 – *Aaron and Joe are released from Beechworth Gaol.*

1877

- 9 January 1877 – *Aaron is arrested for abusing a horse. The following day he is fined £5.*
- 13 January 1877 – *Aaron Sherritt fractures Ah On's skull with a rock during a confrontation*
- 14 January 1877 – *Aaron Sherritt arrested*
- 15 January 1877 – *Joe Byrne arrested*
- 13 February 1877 – *Committal hearing for Ah On case*
- 28 February 1877 – *Trial of Aaron Sherritt and Joe Byrne for unlawful injury deferred.*
- 1 March 1877 – *Aaron and Joe stand trial over the Ah On case. They get off.*
- June 1877 – *Aaron and Joe join Ned Kelly in his horse stealing operation*

1878

- 26 October 1878 – *Ned Kelly, Joe Byrne, Dan Kelly and Steve Hart kill three police in an ambush at Stringybark Creek*
- Late October 1878 – *Aaron Sherritt provides assistance to the Kelly Gang as they attempt to avoid capture*
- 6 November 1878 – *The "Rats' Castle Fiasco"; Aaron Sherritt reaches a verbal agreement with the Chief Commissioner of police to spare Joe Byrne's life if he can get him to hand over the other three bushrangers*
- December 1878 – *The Kelly Gang stick up Younghusband's Station and rob the Second National Bank at Euroa*

1879

- February 1879 – *Aaron visits the police station in Benalla to give information to Captain Standish about Joe Byrne and Dan Kelly visiting* him to recruit him as a scout for an excursion into New South Wales; Standish is absent so Hare is told instead

- 6 February 1879 – *The Kelly Gang raid Jerilderie; They remain until the 10th*
- March 1879 – *Aaron receives a letter from Joe written in code summoning him to a race meeting in Whorouly*
- 2 June 1879 – *Superintendent Hare takes over as head of the hunt for the Kellys*
- 26 June 1879 – *Joe Byrne writes a letter to Aaron requesting a meeting and declaring that sympathisers want him dead*
- *One of the Kellys visits the Sherritt selection at Sheepstation Creek to ask Aaron to accompany them droving near Sandy Creek*
- 2 July – *Aaron goes to the Puzzle Ranges to meet Joe Byrne, reports that Byrne did not show up*
- 15 July 1879 – *Aaron is arrested on a charge of horse stealing filed by Mrs. Byrne*
- 22 July 1879 – *Aaron is committed for trial*
- 26 July 1879 – *Aaron stands trial over the theft of Charlie the horse*
- October 1879 – *Aaron begins courting Ellen Barry (Belle)*
- 6 November 1879 – *Joe Byrne meets with Jack Sherritt to speak with him about scouting for a potential bank robbery in Yackandandah*
- 13 November 1879 – *Dan Kelly visits the Sherritt selection to speak to Jack*
- 23 November 1879 – *Joe Byrne meets with Aaron and Jack Sherritt to announce a change in his bank robbery plans; they are to strike a bank in Beechworth instead of Yackandandah*
- 26 December 1879 – *Aaron Sherritt and Belle Barry are married in Beechworth*

1880

- 3 February 1880 – *Aaron transfers the lease from his selection at Sheepstation Creek to Emma Crawford*
- 3 April 1880 – *The cave party is dissolved*
- 13 May 1880 – *Aaron appears at the Wangaratta Police Court charged with fraud against William Willis*
- 2 June 1880 – *Hare returns to lead the hunt for the Kellys*
- 26 June 1880 – *Aaron Sherritt is murdered by Joe Byrne*
- 28 June 1880 – *Joe Byrne killed by police at Glenrowan; Inquest into Aaron Sherritt's murder begins; Aaron is buried in Beechworth cemetery*
- 30 June 1880 – *Inquest concludes, verdict is that Joe Byrne murdered Aaron Sherritt by shooting*

Aaron Sherritt, photographed by Bray of Beechworth.
[Courtesy: Wikimedia Commons]

Sources

I have spent the better part of twenty-two years studying the Kelly story, so to list every source I have read, viewed or heard in my research would be an impossible task. Instead, I have supplied below a list of some of the key texts that I referred to while writing this book.

There are a great many more sources that you will be able to find with a bit of your own research, but I highly recommend looking at these if you want to verify information that I have included yourself.

Though Ned Kelly is a popular subject for authors, very few give much thought to Aaron Sherritt. To date I have found the research by Ian Jones and Georgina Stones in relation to Aaron Sherritt and Joe Byrne to have been immeasurably beneficial in my own studies, and I have no qualms in stating that in this regard I stand on the shoulders of giants. What I have included in this book is only a fraction of the information that both of those historians have uncovered in their respective research, and I cannot recommend more highly that you seek out their work as well.

- Royal Commission on the Police Force of Victoria. *Police Commission: Minutes of evidence taken before Royal Commission on the Police Force of Victoria, together with appendices* John Ferres, Government Printer Melbourne 1881
- Hare, Francis Augustus. *The Last of the Bushrangers: An Account of the Capture of the Kelly Gang.* ed. London: Hurst and Blackett ltd., 1894.
- Stones, Georgina. "Aaron Sherritt: A Forgotten Life (Part One)." *An Outlaw's Journal*, 17 May 2019, anoutlawsjournal.com/2019/05/17/aaron-sherritt-a-forgotten-life-part-one.

- Jones, Ian. *The fatal friendship: Ned Kelly, Aaron Sherritt and Joe Byrne.* Revised ed. South Melbourne. Lothian books, 2003.
- Kelly, Ned & Byrne, Joe (1879) *Letter written by Joe Byrne at the dictation of Ned Kelly, [1879 Feb.].*
- Sadleir, John. *Recollections of a Victorian Police Officer.* Facsimile ed. Ringwood, Vic: Penguin Australia, 1973. Print. Penguin Colonial Facsimiles.
- Bonwick, James. *Notes of A Gold Digger, And Gold Diggers' Guide.* Melbourne, R. CONNEBEE, 1852, www.gutenberg.org/files/57161/57161-h/57161-h.htm.
- "THE LAND ACT, 1869." *Geelong Advertiser,* 5 January 1870: 3.
- "THE POLICE AND THE KELLY GANG." *The Sydney Daily Telegraph (NSW)* 18 December 1880: 7.
- "HISTORY OF BEECHWORTH." *Ovens and Murray Advertiser,* 28 September 1861: 2.
- "BEECHWORTH POLICE COURT." *Ovens and Murray Advertiser,* 1 March 1870: 2.
- "INQUEST ON AH SUEY." *Ovens and Murray Advertiser,* 10 May 1872: 3.
- " BEECHWORTH POLICE COURT." *Ovens and Murray Advertiser,* 23 September 1873: 2.
- "MURDER OF A CHINESE." *The Age (Melbourne),* 6 May 1874: 3.
- "BEECHWORTH POLICE COURT." *Ovens and Murray Advertiser,* 11 December 1875: 1.
- "BEECHWORTH POLICE COURT." *Ovens and Murray Advertiser,* 3 February 1876: 2.
- "BEECHWORTH POLICE COURT." *Ovens and Murray Advertiser,* 1 June 1876: 4.
- " BEECHWORTH POLICE COURT." *Ovens and Murray Advertiser,* 13 January 1877: 4.
- "BEECHWORTH GENERAL SESSIONS." *Ovens and Murray Advertiser,* 3 March 1877: 1.
- "PRISON REFORM." *The Australasian (Melbourne)* 14 September 1872: 17.
- "THE POLICE MURDERS." *The Argus,* 8 November 1878: 6.
- "THE KELLY GANG FROM WITHIN" *The Sun (Sydney)* 4 September 1911: 10 (LATEST EDITION).
- Ward, Michael Edward, *To the ACP from Detective Michael Ward re: interview with Jack Sherritt* (17 July, 1879) [VPRS 4965 Po UNIT 5 ITEM 61 RECORD 1]
- "A THREATENING LETTER." *Ovens and Murray Advertiser,* 4 September 1879: 2.
- "ALLEGED HORSESTEALING." *The Herald (Melbourne)* 26 July 1879: 3.

- "BEECHWORTH POLICE COURT." *Ovens and Murray Advertiser,* 27 March 1880: 6.
- "WANGARATTA POLICE COURT." *Ovens and Murray Advertiser,* 15 May 1880: 8.
- "HOW WE CAPTURED NED KELLY." *Euroa Advertiser* 11 March 1910: 6.
- "THE INQUEST ON AARON SHERRITT." *Ovens and Murray Advertiser,* 29 June 1880: 2.
- "REUTER'S TELEGRAMS." *Ovens and Murray Advertiser,* 29 June 1880: 2.
- Sherritt, John, *Letter from John Sherritt Sen. after Aaron was murdered.* Francis Hare Papers no.29, 1 July 1880. University of Melbourne Archives.
- "MRS AARON SHERRITT'S ANNUITY." *Ovens and Murray Advertiser.* 23 April 1881: 4.
- "A NOVEL CHARGE." *The Argus (Melbourne)* 5 February 1902: 8.
- "THE POLICE AND THE KELLY GANG." *The Sydney Daily Telegraph (NSW)* 18 December 1880: 7.

Aidan Phelan is the writer and historian for *A Guide to Australian Bushranging*, an online resource that has been bringing Australia's outlaw heritage to a worldwide audience since 2017. In 2020 he published his first novel, *Glenrowan*, which depicts the final months of the Kelly Gang's outlawry. He has also worked as an illustrator and regularly provides illustrations for *An Outlaw's Journal* by Georgina Stones. He is also developing *Glenrowan* as a television miniseries with Matthew Holmes (writer and director of *The Legend of Ben Hall*).

Aidan has a Bachelor of Arts and a Diploma of Education, but also studied writing and editing at what is now known as Melbourne Polytechnic. He was born and raised in the suburbs of Melbourne and developed a fascination with the story of Ned Kelly on his first visit to Glenrowan as a child. This soon grew to be a fully-fledged obsession for a time, eventually culminating in the creation of *A Guide to Australian Bushranging*. The site began life as a repository for the information he had accrued on the subject of colonial banditry, but has since incorporated reviews and articles on related popular culture as well, and he is developing a non-fiction book under the same banner.

www.ingramcontent.com/pod-product-compliance
Lightning Source LLC
Chambersburg PA
CBHW070637150426
42811CB00050B/338